W9-ADV-838

Korea's
Syngman Rhee

1. Syngman Rhee, forced at the age of eighty-five to abdicate the presidency of the Republic of Korea, waves from the porch of his home in Seoul after riding through cheering, weeping crowds into retirement on April 28, 1960. (*Pacific Stars and Stripes Photo*)

Korea's Syngman Rhee

An Unauthorized Portrait

by Richard C. Allen

CHARLES E. TUTTLE COMPANY: PUBLISHERS
Rutland, Vermont Tokyo, Japan

Published by the Charles E. Tuttle Company
of Rutland, Vermont & Tokyo, Japan
with editorial offices at
15 Edogawa-cho, Bunkyo-ku, Tokyo

Library of Congress Catalog
Card No. 60-15606

First edition, 1960

PRINTED IN JAPAN

Contents

List of Illustrations

Foreword

OF ALL the peoples in the world, hardly any has found the road to freedom and human dignity more beset with perils than have the Koreans. For centuries they were victims of their own misrule; then, when the protective hand of China was withdrawn at the end of the nineteenth century, Korea found itself at the mercy first of Japanese militarism and then of Soviet imperialism. For the first half of the twentieth century the Japanese saw to it that Korea remained the Hermit Kingdom. Indeed, the peninsula was effectively blocked off from Western political and philosophical thought until after 1945.

When the Japanese surrender brought the liberation of Korea after World War II, freedom came only to the southern half. Even here, foreign domination was succeeded by domestic turmoil and finally by civil war. For over a decade, Korea was a cold-war pawn in her international relations and a tightly run police state in her domestic affairs. Not until 1960 did the Korean people assume a major voice in the determination of their country's destiny. They could not eject the Communists from the northern half of their homeland, but they could and did move their own half of Korea a step in the direction of political freedom. The future is in the hands of the people of South Korea.

Yet if South Korea is at the threshold of a new era, what of the old? One man spanned the decades between the period of Chinese suzerainty in Korea—through the Japanese occupation and for almost fifteen years following World War II—and the recent revolution. He reached a pinnacle of popularity during the post-liberation period, yet twelve years later was thrown out of office by revolution. The man is Syngman Rhee, who during his own lifetime has become almost a legend in both the East and the West and who, in much of the world, is considered the veritable embodiment of the struggle for Korean independence.

It is always saddening when a patriot is corrupted by the power that comes to him as a gift from his people after a lifetime of service to his country. Yet the same people who demanded the resignation of Syngman Rhee as their president in April of 1960 recalled enough of his earlier services to cheer him as he reluctantly abdicated the absolute authority that he had held for so many years.

The story of South Korea is indeed the story of its erstwhile president, even as the fall of his government can be traced directly to the personal shortcomings of the head of state. In retrospect, Rhee as president had two great failings. One was his ego: his unwillingness to accept criticism and his obsession with his own infallibility. The second was his advanced age, a condition over which he had no control but which underscored his tendencies toward inflexibility and irresponsibility. So formidable were the problems involved in dealing with Korea's irascible patriarch that, when the Korean people finally deposed him of their own volition, the reaction from Washington was one of obvious relief.

Syngman Rhee, in a statement issued from his retirement, has indicated that he awaits vindication by history. He may come to feel, with General Burgoyne in Shaw's *The Devil's Disciple,* that "History, sir, will tell lies, as usual." In any case, the chapters that follow will touch upon a number of areas in which Dr. Rhee can expect the judgment of history to be harsh.

In writing of Rhee and his times, the author has grappled with a problem that must plague anyone who writes on Korea: the transliteration of Korean names. In the Korean language, the surnames Rhee, Lee, and Yi are all written with the same character. But the subject of this work is known throughout the world as Syngman Rhee, and his late political lieutenant was generally known as Lee Ki-bung. The author has therefore used the spelling best known in the West, but has generally placed the surname first (e.g., Kim Il-sung) in accordance with Korean custom.

The author is grateful to the following for their permission to quote from the works cited: Dodd, Mead and Company, *Syngman Rhee: The Man behind the Myth,* by Robert T. Oliver (copyright 1954 by Robert T. Oliver); Harper and Brothers, *From the Danube to the Yalu,* by Mark W. Clark (1954), *The Public Papers and Addresses of Franklin D. Roosevelt, 1942,* edited by Samuel Rosenman (1950), and *Soldier,* by Matthew B. Ridgway (1956); *Harper's Magazine,* "Syngman Rhee: The Free Man's Burden," by Frank Gibney (February 1954); Jacques Chambrun, Inc., *Korean Tales,* by Melvin B. Voorhees (1952); the Louisiana State University Press, *Korea and the Old Orders in East Asia,* by Frederick M. Nelson (1946); The Macmillan Company, *Korea Tomorrow,* by Chung Kyung-cho (1956), and *Memoirs,* by Cordell Hull (1948); the Robert M. McBride Company, *Decision in Korea,* by Rutherford M. Poats (1954); Frederick A. Praeger, Inc., *The Peoples of the Soviet Far East,* by Walter Kolarz (1954); the Fleming H. Revell Company, *Japan Inside Out,* by Syngman Rhee (1944); Time-Life, Inc., *Years of Decision* and *Years of Trial and Hope,* by Harry S. Truman (1955, 1956); the University of Pennsylvania Press, *The Korea Knot,* by Carl Berger (1957); The Viking Press, Inc., *The Forrestal Diaries,* edited by Walter Millis (1951); A. A. Wyn, Inc., *My Forty-Year Fight for Korea,* by Louise Yim (1951); the Council on Foreign Relations, *Korea: A Study of U.S. Policy in the United Nations,* by Leland M. Goodrich (1956); the Institute of Pacific Relations, *Korea Today,* by George M. McCune (1950), *Modern Korea,* by Andrew J. Grajdanzev (1944), and *Source Materials on Korean Politics and Ideologies,* edited by Donald G. Tewksbury; the Ronald Press Company, *The Koreans and Their Culture,* by Cornelius Osgood; the *Christian Science Monitor;* the *New York Times.*

Korea's
Syngman Rhee

1: Syngman Rhee's Korea

GEOGRAPHICALLY, Korea is a mountainous peninsula jutting out from the Asia mainland, slightly larger than the state of Minnesota. Politically it has long been a weak nation surrounded by powerful neighbors, a focal point for the rivalries of China, Japan, and Russia. In recent years Korea has taken on a third, ideological dimension, for in 1950 it became a symbol of the sacrifices the Free World was—and was not—prepared to make in order to contain Communist aggression.

The key to Korea's history, like that of Poland and Belgium, has been its geographic location. A buffer between Japan and the Asia mainland, Korea has borne the brunt of repeated invasions and encroachments by its neighbors. It has been Korea's lot to have its destiny determined by others.

The Koreans themselves are a Mongoloid people numbering about thirty-two million; hence they are about the twelfth largest ethnic group in the world. Today there is little about the Koreans to suggest that theirs was once a flourishing civilization, yet in the fifteenth and sixteenth centuries Korea enjoyed a golden age comparable to any in the East. With the advent of the Yi dynasty came the earliest astronomical tower, the first use of movable metal type, and the successful employment of ironclad warships. Korean influences made themselves felt in the arts and crafts of Japan.

Korea's internal development saw a gradual evolution from separate tribal groups to feudal kingdoms, and finally to a united

Korea under the Silla (57 B.C.—A.D. 935) and Yi (A.D. 1392–1910) dynasties. But the lot of the Korean peasant changed little with Korea's entry into modern times. He works his land today with tools little different from those of his ancestors, and lives in the L-shaped thatched hut which evolved over centuries. While Seoul periodically seethed with intrigue, the Korean farmer generally stuck close to his task of earning subsistence from an overcrowded land. Only recently has he felt the encroachments of a central government; for centuries he had only to tolerate the tax collector who came to take his rice and cloth. Even today the farmer leads his oxcart to market over the same dusty road traversed by his ancestors.

Culturally, the Koreans are notable if only for having successfully resisted cultural assimilation by the Chinese. Almost from the dawn of Korean history China played a major influence in the peninsula, first bringing Buddhism to Korea and later the classical literature of Confucius. But although Korean literature and ceramics were strongly influenced by the Chinese, the Koreans retained their own language and a national identification apart from the Asia mainland.

The flowering of the Yi dynasty ended with the Hideyoshi invasion of 1592, during which the Japanese laid waste to the peninsula before being turned back by a Korean army and its Chinese allies. The Korean court never truly recovered from the shock of Hideyoshi's invasion, and it shortly fell prey to a Manchu invasion from the north. The Korean people suffered patiently the ravages of war, pestilence, and taxation, but peace brought little relief. Corruption became rife in the royal court in Seoul, with Korea's neighbors alternately bribing their way into favor.

Korea's becoming a "hermit kingdom" was a natural result of successive invasions by the Japanese and the Manchus, compounded by a historical distrust of foreigners. Until late in the nineteenth century, Korea's isolation, interrupted as it was only by a few missionaries and wandering voyagers, was even more complete than that of Japan or China. To a greater extent than

2. Syngman Rhee at about the age of twenty. This photograph dates from Rhee's days at the Paichai School, when he and a group of fellow students founded the *Maiyil Sinmun* and Rhee became one of Philip Jaisohn's lieutenants in the newly organized Independence Club. (*Pacific Stars and Stripes Photo*)

the Chinese or Japanese, the Koreans came to distrust their neighbors as well as the West, and xenophobia was a strain which would periodically recur throughout Korea's history.

"The political history of Korea in the nineteenth century," observes Cornelius Osgood, "is essentially that of reaction to the pressures of modern nations."[1] Its system of government, modeled after that of the Ming rulers, had scarcely changed since the inception of the Yi dynasty. The king was in theory an absolute ruler, advised by a three-man cabinet led by the prime minister. By the late nineteenth century, corruption and inefficiency in the royal government encouraged both Japan and Russia to break the centuries-old filial relationship between China and Korea under which the latter paid obeisance to Peking.

Thus it was into a society beset with new pressures from without that Syngman Rhee was born around 1875. His father was a *yangban,* a member of the highest class of society comprised largely of scholars and civil servants. Although Lee Kyung-sun had lost his earlier wealth, his social standing itself was a prized possession in Korea. To this day the yangban draws attention in the Korean countryside: a distinguished figure with his white, flowing gown, characteristic long pipe, and tall horsehair hat.

Rhee's biographer has written that "all his life Syngman Rhee has been more intimately influenced by women than by men."[2] In the Orient the relationship between father and son is often a restrained one, and so it was with Rhee. With his mother, who was also his first teacher, he appears to have been much more close. She taught him from a Chinese reader, and raised him in the tradition of Chinese classicism, a reflection of the extent of Chinese influence in Korea.

Rhee's first contact with the West was a dramatic one. When he was nine, an epidemic of smallpox left him blind in both eyes. His parents sought relief in all of Korea's herb remedies without success. Only as a last resort did they determine to take the young boy to a foreigner: the newly-arrived medical missionary, Dr. Horace Allen.

Dr. Allen was later to become American minister in Seoul, and this would not be the last time his path would cross Syngman Rhee's. To a terrified boy of nine, however, Dr. Allen's medicines restored the gift of sight, and undoubtedly made possible Rhee's later political career. In the afterglow of his restoration, Rhee could scarcely not have been impressed by the fact that Western medicine had cured his blindness when all the old ways had failed.

His experience with Horace Allen may have been the factor that stimulated Rhee to further interest in the West, or it may have been the growing influence of missionaries in Korea. In any case, at the age of nineteen Rhee began attending—at first secretly—the Paichai School, founded by a Methodist minister, Henry G. Appenzeller. There he learned of the Western world and confirmed what his episode of blindness had led him to suspect: that Korea was hopelessly backward and was falling behind even its Eastern neighbors. In his two years at Paichai, Rhee may have first come to think of the West as the power center of the world; late in life he spoke of Paichai as the first school in Korea to provide "full-fledged western education." When their agitation for Korean independence would force them to leave Korea, persons such as Kim Koo and Kim Ok-kun would go to China. Syngman Rhee would go to Washington.[3]

By the last decade of the nineteenth century, the Korean court faced threats from Japan and Russia with an attitude compounded of ignorance and paralysis. A dynasty rendered ineffectual by corruption, nepotism, and lack of leadership continued to look to China for protection while factions oriented towards Japan and Russia jockeyed for position.

When the last of the true Yi kings died in 1864, the son of Prince Tae-won gained the throne after a succession of intrigues stimulated by the absence of a legitimate heir. In an attempt to consolidate his power, Tae-won had himself named regent until his son came of age, at which time he married him to a daughter of the influential Min family. Tae-won reckoned without the strength and political acumen of the queen, however, who was several years older than the new king. Korea's downfall was to be hastened by the maneuverings of the regent and the queen to control the Korean court, and to orient the Hermit Kingdom towards one or another of its powerful neighbors.

In 1885, China and Japan concluded the Tientsin Convention calling for a mutual withdrawal of troops sent to Korea the previous year in the wake of an abortive coup by the Japanese. The agreement provided only a temporary respite, however, for Japan was convinced of China's military weakness and had become increasingly willing to provoke hostilities over Korea. In cooperation with many nationalistic Koreans, Japanese agents in Seoul attempted to undermine the Hermit Kingdom's traditional ties with China.

Although Korea had made treaties as an independent government in the late nineteenth century, Queen Min manifested a strong preference for Chinese advisors, and the court at Seoul continued to reflect the Chinese influence long paramount in Korea. The followers of the ex-regent, Tae-won, were only partially successful in checking Chinese influence. For personal and political reasons Tae-won opposed the queen; the weak king pathetically sought America's aid as a disinterested broker. Ironically, a "progressive" group of government officials looked to Japan as their model and as the instrument by which to counter Chinese influence. Although Paichai had turned Rhee's chief attention across the Pacific, it is possible that at that time he might have preferred increased Japanese influence in Korea to the decadence of the China-oriented Yi dynasty.

In 1894, a rebellion in southern Korea by the Tong Hak, a politico-religious grouping linked to Prince Tae-won, prompted Korea to appeal to China for aid. Peking responded with 1,500 troops; Japan, whose aid was unsolicited, sent nearly 10,000, at the same time claiming that China's failure to advise Japan of its intention to send troops was a violation of the Tientsin Convention. Japanese troops in Seoul seized the king, and China acknowledged the opening of hostilities after the Japanese sank a ship carrying Chinese troops.

The resulting Sino-Japanese War ended in quick victory for the Japanese. The treaty of Shimonoseki seemed innocuous as far as Korea was concerned, since China was forced to recognize, as Japan already had, the full independence and autonomy of Korea. The Hermit Kingdom's close relations with China had irritated the Western powers, and they viewed Japan's victory in the Sino-Japanese War as having provided a needed clarification of Korea's status.[4]

But the dangers of "independence"—in fact, the absence of Chinese protection—became immediately apparent in Seoul, where the king continued a virtual prisoner of the Japanese. In addition, the successful conclusion of the war with China brought increased influence to Japanese militarists unsympathetic toward those moderates who advocated the gradual development of Korea as a Japanese sphere of influence.

An acerbating factor was Queen Min, who had retained her Chinese advisors and was vigorously opposed to the Japanese. On October 8, 1895, Japanese soldiers—apparently in connivance with Korean followers of Tae-won—attacked Duk Soo Palace, threatened the king, and then murdered the queen and the head of the household. The body of the queen was drenched in kerosene and burned.

For months after the murder of Queen Min, the king remained a prisoner in the palace. On February 11, 1896, however, he escaped in disguise to the protection of the Russian Embassy, an action which prompted the Russians to reassert their interest in Korea and which effectively postponed Korea's assimilation by Japan until the obstacle represented by Russia could be removed. Proclaimed the king:

"On account of the unhappy fate of our country, traitors have made trouble every year. Now We have a document informing Us of another conspiracy. We have therefore come to the Russian Legation.

"Soldiers! Come and protect Us! You are Our children. . . . When you meet the chief traitors . . . cut off their heads at once, and bring them here."[5]

To Syngman Rhee, the tug-of-war between the Japanese and the Russians over Korea was less important than the mounting evidence of Korea's inability to defend its own sovereignty. At the Paichai School, Rhee began writing editorials which castigated the government for its failure to implement court reforms and provide for national defense. Then, with a number of fellow students, Rhee bought a printing press and began his own newspaper, the *Maiyil Sinmun.*

At Paichai, therefore, Rhee was doing more than learning of the West. At a time when his education had scarcely begun, he was plunged into the unequal struggle to maintain Korean independence.

2: The Twilight of Independence

BY THE mid-1890's, Korea's chances of maintaining her independence were precarious. She turned from one of her neighbors to another, but each provided protection only in exchange for sovereignty-eroding concessions. It was now Russia's turn to surround the king with its own advisors, and to obtain from the court long-term leases on railroads and mines. The king turned again to the American minister for support, but U.S. interest in Korean independence would be fifty years in coming.

The murder of the queen had heightened the king's fears for his personal safety, and turned him into a virtual recluse. Into the void created by the absence of royal leadership, however, stepped a representative of Korea's increasingly nationalistic middle class.

So Jae-pil, known by his anglicized name Philip Jaisohn, had made common cause during the early 1880's with the Japan-oriented Korean "progressives" who, led by Kim Ok-kun, attempted to induce the Korean court to follow Japan's example in Westernization. In 1884, however, an unsuccessful coup discredited both the Japanese and the Korean progressives and forced Jaisohn to flee to the United States.

In America, Jaisohn earned his M.D. from Johns Hopkins University, the first Korean to do so. He returned to Korea in 1895, however, hoping that the king's escape from the Japanese would provide an opportunity for the reform and strengthening of the monarchy. He joined the staff at Paichai School, which soon became a focal point of Korean nationalism. In 1896 he formed the Independence Club, with Syngman Rhee as one of his lieutenants.

The alleged purpose of the club was "to discuss matters concerning official improvements, customs, laws, religion, and various pertinent affairs in modern lands."[1] In practice, Jaisohn sought to Americanize the Korean government by making it responsive to public opinion. But before tackling the task of creating public opinion, the Independence Club sought to bolster the independence of the feeble monarchy. To the king they petitioned:

"We, Your Majesty's humble servants, desire to state that two important factors constitute an independent and sovereign state, namely: first, it must not lean upon another nation nor tolerate foreign intervention in the national administration; secondly, it must help itself by adopting a wise policy and enforcing justice throughout the realm. The power of establishing these two great principles has been invested to Your Gracious Majesty by Heaven above. Whenever this power is destroyed there is no sovereignty. . . .

"Recently we, your humble servants, have observed that the condition of the nation is on the verge of destruction; great disappointment and constant discontent prevail in the heart of every citizen. The reason for this state of affairs is the giving away of the authority of administering the national finance . . . [and] the military departments. . . . Even the power of appointing and dismissing government officials has been taken from our own authorities.

"The only way to maintain order and achieve improvement in national life is to enforce just laws and apply proper rules and regulations to all institutions of the government. But of late the authorities disregard both the old and the new laws and the rules and regulations have become worthless dead letters. Under such circumstances how can we expect other nations to consider us capable of self government? . . .

"Alas! . . . The consequence is that the most powerful

3. Syngman Rhee (left rear) with a group of classmates and professors at Harvard University in 1908. This was the year in which Rhee was granted a master's degree for his studies in international relations and in which conditions in Korea influenced him to the decision to continue his education abroad. (*Pacific Stars and Stripes Photo*)

neighbors have been treating us as if we are nobody, and even Your Majesty's position has become perilous."[2]

Although the king regarded it with distrust, the Independence Club increased in influence. When, in March 1898, the czar demanded virtual control of the government on penalty of withdrawing his advisors, the club was among the first to urge the king to call Russia's bluff. When the timid king complied, and the Russians indeed withdrew, Korea seemed ready for reforms which Jaisohn hoped would strengthen its prestige abroad. The king hired Jaisohn as a special advisor and appointed a forward-looking new cabinet which included considerable representation from the Independence Club. But the reformists' ascendancy was short-lived. The king's reactionary advisors fed him tales of plots against the monarchy, and in May the king paid Jaisohn for the balance of his contract and dismissed him. On November 5 the king ordered the Independence Club disbanded and its members arrested.

The members of the club scattered, many seeking sanctuary in foreign compounds. Syngman Rhee found refuge in the American Methodist Hospital near South Gate, and remained there even after the king had promised American Minister Horace Allen that no harm would come to the independence leaders. As one of the Independence Club's leading agitators, Rhee had little confidence in the king's word.

One day, however, restless in his confinement, Rhee asked a member of the hospital staff, Dr. Harry C. Sherman, if he might accompany him on his rounds. The doctor assented, but scarcely had the two left the compound when Rhee was spotted, seized by court detectives, and thrown into jail.

In a country where torture has long been an accepted means of police interrogation, Rhee was fortunate in having missionary protectors. His American friends made regular visits to his prison to be sure that he was not being tortured. Minister Allen, a onetime missionary himself, protested the persecution of the Independence Club as being in violation of the king's word.

With such outside aid Rhee's release might well have been secured through pressure on the court. In the course of a visit, however, one of Rhee's colleagues rashly passed him a pistol. An escape plan was arranged whereby Rhee and two others would force their way out of prison and then seek the protection of a pro-independence crowd outside the prison. Brandishing the pistol, the three made good their escape, but because of confusion in the timing no crowd was in the square, and only one of the three was able to make his way to a foreign compound and avoid recapture.[3]

When Rhee was returned to prison, it was the beginning of seven years' incarceration—years which would see the death of the Independence Club, the further deterioration of the monarchy, and a supplanting of Russian influence in Korea by the ubiquitous Japanese. To Rhee personally, his prison years would mean an end to his early marriage, which had been arranged by his parents and consummated in 1896.* But his term in prison would also go far in hardening his resolve to continue to work for Korean independence.

For the first seven months of his prison term Rhee received standard Korean treatment at the hands of his jailors. Hours of physical torture alternated with periods of dampness and filth in prison isolation. According to his biographer, two sticks would be placed between Rhee's legs; his legs were then bound tightly together and the sticks twisted. Sharp pieces of bamboo were tied between his fingers and his hand tightened until flesh sheared from the bone. For hours at a time he was clamped into stocks, with a 20-pound canque of wood around his neck so that he could neither sit nor stand.[4] Nonetheless Rhee took everything his tormenters

* Robert T. Oliver, *Syngman Rhee: The Man behind the Myth* (New York, 1954), pp. 52–53. According to Oliver, Rhee's first wife was somewhat older than he but was "distinguished by unusual strength of intellect and character." Oliver acknowledges that her fate is "uncertain" but states that she bore him a son who died in Philadelphia in 1908 after being sent to America to study. It has been periodically rumored that Rhee's first wife is still alive, pensioned off in a province of southern Korea.

could offer, and when he became president of South Korea these and some additional refinements would be used on his own political opponents.

When Rhee was finally brought to trial, he might well have received a death sentence. Several factors, however, worked in his favor: the circumstances of his original apprehension, which prompted Rhee's missionary friends to maintain that his being with Dr. Sherman implied immunity from arrest; Minister Allen's known partiality for the Independence Club, which he freely expressed to the king, with whom he was a favorite; and finally the fact that it was not Rhee but Choe Chong-sik, who had been apprehended with him at the time of the escape, who was most wanted by the royal court. At the trial Choe was sentenced to death, Rhee to life imprisonment.

Rhee's incarceration coincided with an ominous new trend in Korea's international affairs. Japan, quick to take advantage of Russia's embarrassment when the Yi king asked for the withdrawal of Russian advisors, concluded with Russia the Nishi-Rosen agreement pledging each to consult the other with respect to the appointment of advisors to the Korean government. More importantly, Russia pledged not to hinder Japan's expanding commercial interests in Korea. Mutual acknowledgment of Korea's "entire independence" suggested that Japan was prepared to try new tactics in connection with the country.

The years leading to the Russo-Japanese War of 1904–5 were marked by accelerated economic imperialism by the Japanese. After Japan had been twice thwarted in attempts to seize control by force, Tokyo's use of the velvet glove proved effective in the end. In July 1898, Japan gained concessions to build one railroad from Seoul to Pusan and another from Seoul to Inchon. In August, Minister Allen reported that strategic property near the treaty ports had been largely bought up by the Japanese, and that many Japanese citizens were residing in the interior of Korea in violation of agreements limiting foreigners to the treaty ports.[5]

Russia's attempts to check the Japanese met with little success.

By 1903, however, tensions arising from conflicting timber claims along the Yalu River had brought Russo-Japanese relations near the breaking point. Militarists in Japan called for war, and the following year brought the conflict which established a Japanese protectorate over the Hermit Kingdom.

By the time of his trial Rhee's darkest hour had passed. In addition to his life sentence he was to have received one hundred blows with a bamboo rod. But the judge left the chamber, and the guard was friendly. Rhee was spared.

In prison Rhee once again benefited from the attention of American missionaries, who brought him food and reading matter. Both the warden and his assistant befriended him, and the hard labor which was to have been part of the sentence was quickly forgotten. For Rhee, as for many another revolutionary, prison proved to be a period of activity and dedication.

Considering the favors Rhee had received from American Methodists in Korea, it is scarcely surprising that prison brought about his conversion to that faith. In 1904, he wrote of his earlier belief:

"It must be remembered that the great ambition which led me to the [Paichai] school was to learn English, and English only. This ambition I quickly achieved, but I soon discovered I was learning something of far greater importance than the English language. I was imbibing ideas of political equality and liberty....

"Then I began to understand that political changes do not come by themselves and are not only a question of laws and regulations. There must also come deep and abiding changes within the hearts and minds of the people—and particularly in the ruling class. I began to listen a little bit to the morning services in the chapel and when I listened I heard that Jesus was more than a symbol of salvation in afterlife. He was also a Great Teacher who brought a gospel of brotherly love and service. I began to have more respect for these foreign religious teachings and in my own private mind I began to consider that maybe Jesus deserved to rank somewhere near Confucius. But further than this I could not or would not go."[6]

Thus prison completed a conversion already underway. Although Rhee's later life has underscored the contradiction between Rhee the Christian minister-teacher and Rhee the political leader, he was to be closely associated with various forms of Christian activity for much of his career. As with everything else, however, his religious work took a back seat to a lifetime of agitation for Korea.

As Rhee's prison lot improved, he was able to resume his political writing. Editorials for the revived *Maiyil Sinmun* were smuggled from the prison and printed anonymously, but the background of their authorship soon became known. They were read by Lady Um, consort to the King and sometime supporter of reform movements in Korea, who encouraged the warden to be lenient to Rhee and his associates. By the traditional Korean means of having a friend in court, Rhee's lot was eased, and he was encouraged to pursue his writing further.

When Rhee turned to composing a book to propagate Korean independence, he found a small but enthusiastic audience. The corruption and weakness of the Korean court were recognized by progressive Koreans, but the dissolution of the Independence Club had left them dispirited and without leadership. The absence of progressives such as Philip Jaisohn, in America, and Kim Okkun, in Shanghai, tended to enhance the popularity of hitherto secondary leaders such as Rhee.

The resulting literary effort, *The Spirit of Independence*, was largely a collection of political essays and admonitions, with chapters dealing with subjects as diverse as astronomy, "stubborn" China, America's Declaration of Independence, and the "foundations of true loyalty." Rhee has acknowledged: "I wrote . . . with very few reference materials, and . . . addressed it in very simple terms to the Korean people, most of whom are uneducated and without any earlier knowledge of the Western world." Although

Rhee's own formal Western education was limited to his two years at Paichai, it is significant that even in his twenties he found himself preaching the gospel of independence to people willing to listen. He wrote:

"If your own heart is without patriotism, your heart is your enemy. You must struggle against your own feelings if they urge you to forgo the struggle for the common cause. Let us examine our hearts now, at this moment. If you find within yourself any single thought of abandoning the welfare of your country, tear it out. Do not wait for others to lead or to do what must be done, but arouse yourself. . . .

"As I have indicated before, to live in this nation is comparable to being a passenger on a ship in a cruel sea. How can you be so indifferent as not to be concerned with the affairs of your own nation, but to insist they are the business of high officials? . . .

"The relationship between you and your nation may seem so remote that you have little reason to love it or to make efforts to save it. Therefore, two enemies must be guarded against: first, the people who try to destroy the nation; and second, those who sit passively by, being without any hope or sense of responsibility."[7]

Thus Rhee appears not to have been pressing a specific program of reform, but rather to have been attempting to awaken his countrymen to the peril from abroad. *The Spirit of Independence* has had none of the impact abroad of other prison-inspired volumes, but in Korea, where independence was itself a new concept to a people long used to Chinese suzerainty, the work was not without significance despite its small distribution.

There were other independence leaders in Seoul Prison besides Rhee, and several would be associated with Rhee at various times after their release. Lee Chung-hyuk would accompany him to the United States in 1904 to plead Korea's cause in America. Park Young-man would become a rival of his among American-oriented Koreans in Hawaii. Hugh Cynn, a boyhood friend of Rhee's, would oppose him for the South Korean presidency in 1952.

The beginning of the Russo-Japanese War in 1904 stirred hopes among the prisoners that a political amnesty would follow Korea's declaration of neutrality, but court reactionaries were not anxious to be troubled again by rabble-rousing young reformers. Some persons in government circles interpreted the United States—Korean friendship treaty of 1882 as guaranteeing American protection against aggression. Minister Allen had indeed assured the king as late as 1900 that "the treaty powers would assist Korea in time of distress, by their good offices, and recalled to his mind the fact that in 1894, at the time of the Sino-Japanese War, when he had asked the good offices of the United States, he had not asked in vain."[8] To the Koreans, accustomed to their earlier Confucian relationship with China, no "big brother" would allow niceties concerning the definition of good offices to prevent him from aiding "little brother."

Even prior to the end of the Sino-Japanese War, Japan had all but assimilated the Hermit Kingdom. A protocol was signed pledging Korea to accept Japanese "improvements in administration." This entering wedge was followed with demands for the abolition of Korea's department of posts and telegraphs, for the placing of Japanese police in every province, for the recall of Korean legations abroad, and finally for indemnity for every Japanese killed by Koreans in the ten years before. When a declaration of amnesty brought Rhee's release on August 9, 1904, his country was a Japanese protectorate in all but name.

One cannot help wondering if Rhee's lifelong hatred of the Japanese does not stem in part from his realization of how skillfully they had made use of Korea's fledgling independence movement to neutralize Russia and accomplish their own ends. But his time in prison had not tempered his zeal for Korean independence. Upon his release, Rhee contracted two progressive ministers of the court, Prince Min Yong-hwan and General Hahn Kyu-sul. He found both concerned over Japanese encroachments and anxious to make a personal appeal to the United States. With the emperor virtually immobilized by Japanese surveillance (the Yi king had assumed the imperial title in 1897 for reasons of prestige), there seemed little possibility of the appointment of an official delegation. It was therefore determined that Rhee would go to Washington, accompanied by his erstwhile prison colleague, Lee Chunghyuk. Theirs would be one of several fruitless missions.

When Rhee left for America in November 1904, he left behind him much of his Korean heritage. His mother had died prior to his imprisonment, and his gradual Westernization had contributed to his estrangement from his Korean wife. Upon his departure he adopted the anglicized name of Syngman Rhee, never to revert to the Korean Lee Sung-man. Yet if his thinking was to be greatly influenced by the West, his lifelong goal had already been determined by the political struggles of his youth—by independence demonstrators waving banners in the streets of Seoul.

3: The Common Enemy

AS SYNGMAN Rhee watched Korea's west coast fade into the horizon from the deck of the *S. S. Ohio* he was hopeful that, away from the historic rivalries of north Asia, Korea might find an ally and protector in the United States. Was there not the treaty of 1882 pledging "amity and friendship" between the Korean and the American peoples? Had not Minister Allen included the United States among treaty powers who stood prepared to use good offices on behalf of Korea?

In fact, however, Rhee's mission was foredoomed. In the United States the Roosevelt administration was actively interested in a settlement of the Russo-Japanese War, but largely in terms of the prestige which would accrue to the United States through the proffering of its good offices. In any case, President Roosevelt looked with favor on the Japanese, while the decadence of the Korean court encouraged a general belief that Japanese rule would benefit the Korean people.

Even apart from these extenuating circumstances, it was hardly realistic to expect that an America still shackled by nineteenth-century isolationism would be willing to guarantee the independence of a country unknown to most of its people and unrelated to its national interest. Syngman Rhee, however, knew little of either American diplomacy or popular attitudes. If there was any hope for Korea in 1904, it had to be the United States. Great Britain had recognized Japan's "special interests" in north Asia the previous year. China had long since been eliminated as a guarantor of Korean independence, and now Russia was on the verge of a humiliating defeat at the hands of the Japanese.

In Hawaii and Los Angeles, Rhee was welcomed by Korean nationalists, and various American missionaries lent encouragement. But the Roosevelt administration in Washington, assuming the role of peacemaker between Japan and Russia, had come to view Korea less as a sovereign state than as the legitimate spoils of victory, a factor capable of manipulation in the peace settlement. Into this situation Rhee brought a crusading zeal for his country and a single-minded belligerence that made it remarkable that he got as far as Oyster Bay.

Rhee arrived with letters of introduction to Senator Hugh A. Dinsmore of Arkansas, a one-time American minister in Seoul who had maintained an interest in Korea and who arranged an interview with Secretary of State John Hay. Characteristically, Rhee interpreted Hay's assurances that the U.S. was mindful of its treaty as a guarantee of American support.

Rhee had left Lee Chung-hyuk in Los Angeles, but in Washington he was joined by Yoon Pyung-ku, a Honolulu minister who along with Rhee had been chosen by Koreans in Hawaii to petition Theodore Roosevelt on behalf of their country. After calling on Philip Jaisohn in Philadelphia, Rhee and Yoon journeyed to Oyster Bay, where they were received by Roosevelt on the eve of the Portsmouth conference. The president, effusing enthusiasm and protestations of friendship for Korea, saw them briefly. He declined to accept a written petition, however, on grounds that it should be sent through diplomatic channels.[1]

As far as its having any effect on Korea's fate was concerned, Rhee's mission was a failure. Even before he saw Roosevelt, William Howard Taft was en route to Tokyo to sign an agreement acknowledging Japan's interests in Korea. But Rhee did not know this.

In Washington, Rhee continued to receive backing from a number of Protestant clergymen, some of whom had heard favorable accounts of him from colleagues in Seoul. For a time, Rhee considered attending a theological seminary. He probably recognized, however, that full-time ministerial duties would allow little time for political activity. In addition, his academic interests were outside the range of the usual theological curriculum.

Although he entered George Washington University on a ministerial scholarship in February 1905, he continued to devote much of his time to agitation on behalf of Korea. Little is known of Rhee's activities in this period, but that he was a source of annoyance to American officials is suggested by a comment from Minister Allen in Seoul, who wrote apologetically to Senator Dinsmore: "I refused to give Ye Sung Mahn a letter to a single person in America and tried to keep him from going."[2]

At George Washington, Rhee's subjects included English, European and American history, and philosophy. Although he had been admitted as a sophomore in recognition of his studies in Seoul, his marks were generally indifferent. The foreign student is recognized as often being at a disadvantage in an American university, but Rhee's mediocre record is not without some significance. Although he would later earn a Ph.D. at Princeton, and at the height of his political career would prefer the title of "Doctor" to that of "President," little in Rhee's career shows him as a profound thinker. Rather, his early career is marked by single-minded devotion to an ideal—Korean independence—and hostility towards every peril, real or imagined, which threatened this ideal.

Rhee supported himself at George Washington through lectures on "Korea, Land of the Morning Calm." But in his homeland the struggle to resist the Japanese was in its final throes. The Portsmouth treaty in September 1905 brought general recognition of Japan's "paramount" interest in Korea. Horace Allen, lobbying for Korea in Washington since his replacement as American minister, regretfully returned his operating funds to the Yi emperor with the remark that the cause was hopeless. In November 1905, Tokyo spelled out its demands for a virtual protectorate over Korea. At first the emperor refused to consent, but when the palace was surrounded by Japanese soldiers, when government ministers were beaten, and when the emperor himself was threatened, the Japanese emerged with the imperial signature.

In a final gesture, the emperor sent a new appeal to the United States, telling Roosevelt that the protectorate had been agreed to under duress. To convey the message he chose Homer B. Hulbert, a Seoul missionary and editor, who agreed to make a secret trip to Washington. In America, however, Hulbert was able to see neither the president nor the secretary of state; the American position was that since the protectorate had been established, the emperor could not make his own representations. The fact was that the last years of the Yi dynasty had been so ineffectual that few Americans, outside of court favorites such as Allen and Hulbert, were sympathetic to the emperor. Most foreigners in Seoul looked with favor on the protectorate, while international opinion had been conditioned by the reports of observers such as George Kennan:

"The Korean Government . . . [comprises] (a) the Emperor's Cabinet, consisting of nine ministers; (b) the sorcerers, soothsayers, fortunetellers, and mudangs or spirit mediums, who influence and often control legislation; (c) the governors of the thirteen provinces; and (d) the magistrates or prefects of the 344 prefectures into which the provinces are divided. All the official positions in classes (c) and (d) are nominally filled by Imperial appointment, but the selection of appointees is subject to court influence, "pull," or intrigue, and, as a rule, the offices are sold to the highest bidder. Provincial governors pay from ten thousand to forty thousand Korean dollars for their places, and then not only recoup themselves but amass fortunes by robbing the defenseless people whom they are sent to govern. As there are no independent law courts, and as every governor or prefect is a judge as well as an administrator, a Korean who is robbed must seek redress from the robber. . . .

"The activities and operations of the existing Korean Government may briefly be summarized as follows: it takes from the people, directly and indirectly, everything that they earn over and above a bare subsistence, and gives them in return practically nothing. It affords no adequate protection to life or property; it provides no educational facilities that deserve notice; it builds no roads; it does not improve its harbors; it does not light its coasts; it pays no attention whatever to streetcleaning or sanitation; it takes no measures to prevent or check epidemics; . . . it corrupts and demoralizes its subjects by setting them examples of untruthfulness, dishonesty, treachery, cruelty, and a cynical brutality in dealing with human rights that is almost without parallel in modern times.*

As significant as Kennan's excoriation of the Korean government was the fact that his judgment of the Korean people gave little hope of reform from within:

"The first impression that the Korean people make upon an impartial and unprejudiced newcomer is strongly and decidedly unfavorable. . . . The domestic environment and personal habits of the lower classes are filthy and repulsive in the extreme; the moony expressionless faces of the petty officials and gentlemen of leisure who saunter through the streets fanning themselves or smoking long-stemmed pipes show no signs of character or traces of experience; and the unemployed workingmen in dirty white cotton jackets and baggy trousers, who lie here and there on the ground with flies crawling over their closed eyelids, do not compare at all favorably with the neat, alert, industrious laborers of Japan. . . .

"As one's field of observation widens, so as to take in country as well as town, and to include moral as well as physical and intellectual characteristics, one's first impressions harden and one's bad opinion of the people settles into a conviction. . . . They are the rotten product of a decayed Oriental civilization."[3]

* Andrew J. Grajdanzev, *Modern Korea* (New York, 1944), pp. 34–35. Kennan, a close friend of Theodore Roosevelt, was the uncle of America's erstwhile ambassador to the Soviet Union and was frequent contributor to *Outlook,* the magazine in which this article appeared.

If Kennan was not an entirely impartial observer, articles such as his nonetheless made it difficult for Rhee to get much sympathy for his country in the United States. Moreover, it was true that when the Japanese resident-general arrived in Seoul in 1906, most foreigners there welcomed the change. Rhee graduated from George Washington in the spring of 1907, shaken by Korea's fate and uncertain as to his own future. Although committed to the Methodist Mission Board to return to Korea on its behalf, he determined to do postgraduate work in the United States and was admitted to Harvard University.

At Harvard Rhee lived in seclusion, "forming no lasting friendships while there and entering not at all into the social life of the college."[4] His academic work improved, however, and he began to read extensively in international relations. When he received his master's degree in the spring of 1908, unstable conditions in his homeland reinforced his new-found academic interests and prompted him to continue his education. At first Rhee decided to do graduate work at Columbia. At the last minute, however, a friend persuaded him to enroll at Princeton.

Rhee's two years at Princeton appear to have influenced him more than any of his previous schooling. The president of Princeton at that time was Woodrow Wilson, whose later eloquence on behalf of national self-determination Rhee would often cite. As at Harvard, Rhee was withdrawn from the student body, but he became a faculty favorite. He attracted the attention of Wilson himself, who provided him with a letter of recommendation for speaking engagements which cited him as "a man of strong patriotic feeling and of great enthusiasm for his people."[5]

Rhee received his doctorate in 1910, the year in which Japan formally annexed its Korean protectorate. By this time the Japanese were well on their way to making Korea a case study in the reprehensible aspects of colonialism. While humiliating the Korean people at every turn, they went about their plan to turn Korea into a major supplier of food and raw materials to their home islands. Physical improvements made by the Japanese were of little benefit to the Koreans; railroad construction was to facilitate the movement of exports to ports such as Inchon and Pusan, and sanitary measures were to make Seoul habitable for Japanese officials. As for the Koreans, it was already apparent that seldom had they ever been united *for* anything as they were united *against* the Japanese.

Even prior to annexation there were uprisings among the politically volatile Koreans. An insurrection by a partisan "Righteous Army" in 1906 was not brought under control for two months. The abdication of the emperor the following year brought riots and demonstrations in Seoul. In 1909, a young Korean nationalist assassinated the Japanese resident-general, Prince Ito, in Harbin. From July 1907 to the end of 1908, according to Japanese figures, nearly 15,000 Korean insurgents were killed and nearly 9,000 taken prisoner.

Japan's formal annexation of Korea came as something of an anticlimax. The Japanese made the abdicated emperor a prince in their own imperial household and bought off leading members of the Korean court with large monetary grants. But beneath the new trappings Korea was under the absolute control of a governor-general who was responsible only to the Japanese emperor and whose centralized control reached down to the smallest county and village.

Although Korea would have presented problems to the most skillful colonizer, so heavy-handed were the Japanese that they succeeded in unifying Korean nationalist sentiment after Korea's own nationalists had failed. Japanese economic exploitation was so overt that it could be recognized as such by the simplest Korean peasant. The scheme of a group of officially backed Japanese financiers to monopolize Korea's underdeveloped land came in for bitter criticism after a number of tracts of land had been turned over at a fraction of their actual value.

Measures aimed at destroying Korea as a national entity were an unnecessary aggravating factor. Under the Japanese the Korean language was dropped from the school curriculum. Koreans were forced to adopt not only Japanese citizenship but also Japanese names. When he became president of South Korea, one of Rhee's major concerns would be measures to preserve the country as a cultural and national entity in the face of any future encroachments by the Japanese and the Russians.

In the period immediately following his graduation from Princeton, Rhee appears to have seriously considered abandoning his role as patriot-in-exile. With Korea's political fortunes at a nadir, Rhee's missionary friends urged him to devote himself to church work. Rhee himself, having enjoyed his years in America, found it difficult to dispute those who pictured the fruitlessness of agitating for a lost national cause.

With mixed emotions Rhee finally accepted a job with the Seoul Y.M.C.A., a step which required his returning to live under Japanese rule. On his return to Korea in the winter of 1910, via Europe and Russia, he moved into the Rhee family home with his father. Although presumably under surveillance by the Japanese, Rhee was not molested.

Rhee might have continued in social work in his homeland but for his fears in connection with Japanese harassment of Korean Christians. By the fall of 1911, rumors were rife that, as part of the Japanese campaign to stamp out foreign influence, Christian churches in Korea would have their charters revoked and be placed under Japanese administration. With little warning, 135 leading Korean Christians were arrested on charges of a "conspiracy" to assassinate the governor-general.

Pressure from Western church circles forced reduction of the severe sentences which had been meted out to the Korean churchmen, but Rhee, fearful that he might be next, determined to leave Korea for good. He left his homeland with probably little hope of seeing it again, but with recognition that as long as Korea remained under the Japanese he would be far better off in the West.

Not long after Woodrow Wilson reached the White House, his doctrines of self-determination became known in Korea, where the Fourteen Points served to remind the people of a national

4. Syngman Rhee (right front) with a group of students at Princeton University in 1910, the year in which Rhee received his doctorate and Japan formally annexed Korea. It was at Princeton that Rhee became a faculty favorite and attracted the attention of Woodrow Wilson, who cited him as "a man of strong patriotic feeling and of great enthusiasm for his people." (*Pacific Stars and Stripes Photo*)

heritage dissipated by Korea's own rulers. In addition, the death of the deposed emperor in January 1919 gave rise to a surge of patriotic feeling. Whatever the shortcomings of the Yi dynasty, it had at least meant rule of Korea by Koreans.

On March 1, 1919, thirty-three leading Koreans met in the Bright Moon Cafe in Seoul, where they signed a declaration of Korean independence which was then read to crowds in the street. Demonstrations spread from Seoul to the countryside, with marching crowds waving long-concealed Korean flags and chanting: "*Mansei!*" (May Korea live ten thousand years!) To underscore the peaceful character of the demonstrations, and with the hope of bringing world opinion to bear on the Japanese, the signatories of the declaration immediately surrendered themselves to the Japanese. Although there were some cases of Korean-instigated violence, the peaceful character of the demonstrations was generally maintained.

The Japanese reaction to the Mansei uprising was swift and cruel. According to Japanese figures, 553 Koreans were killed, over 1,400 wounded, and over 10,000 flogged. In retrospect, prospects for outside intervention were so poor in 1919 that the uprising was clearly ill-timed. The armistice had taken its toll of the Wilsonian idealism which had marked the war years, while Japan had emerged from the war with sufficient prestige that none of the Allies were anxious to antagonize Tokyo. When Rhee had sought to lobby for Korea at Versailles in 1918, he had been refused an American passport lest his presence there embarrass the Japanese.*

To the Koreans, the dignity which marked the nation-wide passive resistance has given it a special place in Korean history. In both its peaceful character and the popular backing it received, the Mansei uprising was a high point in the Korean independence

* Although Rhee was in the United States at the time of the Mansei uprising and played no role in the events of 1919, spokesmen for the Rhee government encouraged references to him as a "leader" of the revolt. When Rhee was forced to abdicate in 1960, at least one wire service story characterized him as having led the 1919 uprising.

movement. Henceforth the independence movement would be noteworthy not for its unity but for its factionalism. Foreign influences, particularly communism, would sap the movement of its purely nationalistic aspect. In the place of passive resistance, violence would become a hallmark of Korean exiles.

The aftermath of the uprising, however, was noteworthy for the formation of a provisional Korean government. A group of independence leaders, meeting in Seoul in April 1919, formed a Korean Provisional Government with Syngman Rhee as president. Although the Provisional Government had not in any sense been elected by the Korean people, appointment of Rhee as its president was recognition of his growing stature in the independence movement. His role in the new government provided a quasi-official basis for his diplomatic representations on behalf of Korea over the next three decades.

The Provisional Government began as essentially a triumvirate of Kim Koo, Ahn Chang-ho, and Rhee, although as time went on, others would play an increasing role. Kim, as premier, established close links with the Chinese Nationalists, and in the 1930's strongly supported Sino-Korean guerrilla activities against the Japanese, while directing assassinations which made him, among the Japanese, the most feared of all Korean exiles. Ahn Chang-ho, leader of the Western-oriented Young Korea Academy (Hungsadan) faction, spent much of his time in Hawaii but was closely associated with underground activity in Korea itself until his death in 1939. Rhee, who was popularly regarded as being on friendly terms with President Wilson, operated largely in the United States. The Provisional Government was controlled from Shanghai, and tended to reflect more the leadership of Kim Koo than of Rhee.

Rhee had left Korea in the spring of 1912, with his nomination as Korean delegate to a Methodist convention in Minneapolis providing him passage. There he first manifested a lifelong penchant for using any available forum for political purposes by delivering a ringing denunciation of the Japanese, which drew severe criticism for endangering missionary activities which had to be carried on under the occupation.[6]

Rhee could not earn a living from his speeches, however, and in 1913 accepted a job as principal of a Korean-language school in Hawaii. The islands would be his home until shortly prior to World War II; they would also be the breeding ground for rivalries—both within and without the framework of the Provisional Government—which would largely dominate post-liberation politics in Korea. In Hawaii as well as in Washington, Rhee would earn his reputation as the stormy petrel of Korean independence.

4: The Politics of Exile

THE PERIOD of the Japanese occupation sent many Koreans away from their homeland. Gradually there came to be three major centers of Korean exiles: the Maritime Province of the U.S.S.R., northern China, and the United States. All three, together with Korea itself, were centers of independence activities. The importance of the expatriate groups is measured by the fact that after liberation both north and south Korea would be largely ruled by erstwhile expatriates.

Within the United States and its territories, no place was more a hotbed of exile activity than Hawaii. Many Asian immigrants to America had gotten no further than Hawaii; there were Japanese, Chinese, and Koreans, some of whom had run out of money in Hawaii, others of whom had been won over by the attractions of living among their fellow nationals in the islands. If the Korean community in Hawaii was not the largest in size, it nonetheless reflected more than any other group the turbulence in its homeland.

Politically conscious Koreans have historically found difficulty in working harmoniously together. Indeed, when Syngman Rhee was beginning his revolutionary career in the Independence Club he had refused a request by Philip Jaisohn to suspend publication of the *Maiyil Sinmun* lest it compete with the club organ *Independence*. A tendency towards factionalism long prevalent in Korean politics was nowhere more in evidence than among exiles in Hawaii, who brought old feuds with them from Korea and developed new ones in the islands. By 1913, the Korean community there was already marked by divisions based on family ties, personal animosities, and provincial origins.

Rhee arrived in Hawaii full of plans for stimulating nationalism among the Koreans there. His post as principal of a Korean-language school, however, brought him into conflict with Methodist authorities over the issue of segregated schools. Although church officials opposed separate schools for different nationalities, Rhee fought for segregation as a means of propagating Korean nationalism. Opposition from church leaders prompted Rhee to break with the Methodists in 1916 and set up his own institution, the Christian Institute, along the lines he had advocated.

Rhee's differences with church authorities were not confined to the educational field. Once having broken with the Methodists, he set up a rival church as he had set up a school, establishing the former as a non-denominational institution dedicated to Korean independence. By striking out on his own when unable to win over his opponents, Rhee became known for his intolerance and impetuousness. His admiring biographer concedes that Rhee's twenty-five years in Hawaii "were marked by disputation."[1] But by setting up his own institutions Rhee was able to build up a strong personal following, some of which would follow him back to Korea in 1945.

The Mansei uprising and the subsequent formation of the Provisional Government prompted Rhee to journey to Washington in the spring of 1919. Just as he had been prevented from pleading Korea's case at Versailles, so was he unable to gain American recognition of the Provisional Government. While in Washington, however, he established a "shadow" Korean legation, the Korean Commission, which was to lobby on behalf of the Provisional Government and Rhee for the next three decades.

The establishment of a government-in-exile, however poor its prospects, served to acerbate differences among independence leaders scattered abroad. In Hawaii, Rhee quarreled with Ahn Chang-ho, head of the well-established Korean National Association and father of the Western-oriented Young Korea Academy. Ahn, like Rhee a Christian and an erstwhile member of the Independence Club, was less interested in immediate political action than in stressing moral values to the Korean people, propagating Korean culture, and introducing Western methods into his homeland. Ahn and his followers, unlike Rhee, were willing to work under the Japanese, and were able to establish schools which served as forums for their teachings and as cover for other independence activities.

If Rhee's relations with his colleagues in Hawaii were less than harmonious, his dealings with the Provisional Government in Shanghai became equally strained. The Provisional Government reflected the fiery leadership of Kim Koo, who sought means of harassing the Japanese militarily and had little respect for Rhee's diplomatic representations. Other elements of the government-in-exile were Communist-inclined and, though distrusted by both Kim and Rhee, pressed vigorously for military cooperation with the Chinese Communists. The Kuomintang's break with the Communists in 1924 hastened the splintering of the Provisional Government into rightist and leftist groups.

Although the exile government remained a predominantly rightist organization, Rhee had no more sympathy with Kim's militant views than with Ahn Chang-ho's program of internal reforms. Rhee's relations with Ahn were further aggravated when Kim Kyu-sic, a leading member of the Young Korea Academy, began to press for the admission of leftists into the Provisional Government. Although his own diplomatic overtures had proven unproductive, Rhee was totally unsympathetic with any approach except his own. Despite Kim Koo's efforts, military activity against the Japanese came to be the province of leftist Koreans.

The Mansei uprising was a purely nationalistic demonstration against Japanese colonialism. Despite Communist propaganda to the contrary, it was neither a proletarian uprising nor one inspired by the Bolshevik revolution. There was nothing proletarian about the signers of the March declaration, who were largely teachers, Christian pastors, and professional men. They had little knowledge of events in Russia, where in any case the success of the Bolsheviks was not yet assured.

By 1920, however, Communist philosophy was winning Korean adherents in the U.S.S.R. and Manchuria. During the Russian Revolution the large concentration of Koreans around Vladivostok had supported Kerensky's provisional government, but after the war the Soviets succeeded in winning over many young Koreans and new immigrants. Although they understood little of the Marxist dialectic, young Koreans who were sufficiently anti-Japanese to have left their homeland were immediately attracted by the Soviets' anti-imperialist professions. These Russian-oriented Koreans would form the nucleus of Communist government in North Korea after World War II.

Gradually, despite harsh Japanese countermeasures, the first Communist cells worked their way into Korea itself. Although the movement appears to have had little direction from Moscow, it found supporters among intellectuals disillusioned with the failure of the peaceful Mansei uprising. In addition, it enjoyed a measure of prestige as a result of the gradual stabilization of the Soviet government. Unity and direction, however, were badly lacking; the factionalism which characterized Korean political activity elsewhere was no worse than that among the Communists. Japanese suppression was severe; large-scale arrests in 1925 and 1926 deprived the party of top leaders such as Pak Hun-young and Choi Chang-ik. Only two years after recognizing the Korean Communist Party the Comintern lamented:

"The ranks of the Communist Party in Korea have in the past consisted almost exclusively of intellectuals and students. A Communist Party built on such foundations cannot be a consistently bolshevik and organizationally sound Party. The first task of the communist movement of Korea is therefore to strengthen its own ranks. . . . The petty-bourgeois intellectual composition of the Party, and the lack of contact with the workers, have hitherto constituted one of the main causes of the permanent crisis in the

5. Syngman Rhee (second row, seventh from left) pictured with members of the Shanghai Provisional Government at a New Year celebration in 1922. This documentary photograph carries black arrows indicating Rhee and Kim Koo (front row, third from left), the latter of whom was killed in 1949 by a Korean Army lieutenant, reportedly a member of Kim's own Korean Independence Party. (*Pacific Stars and Stripes Photo*)

communist movement of Korea. The frequent failures of the Korean communists show that the Party was unable to organize its conspiratorial work properly."[2]

Korea's domestic Communists were so nationalistic in outlook that Moscow may never have reposed much confidence in them. But for Korea, unlike China, the Soviets were able to develop leadership from among Russian-raised nationalists who in time would make North Korea the most responsive and submissive of Soviet satellites.

Also susceptible to Communist indoctrination were Koreans who had migrated to China and Manchuria. But these areas became a haven for Koreans of all extremes, whether right or left, and the facts of geography made them less susceptible to Soviet influence than to Chinese. China-oriented Koreans were particularly successful in harassing the Japanese during the 1930's. A Japanese account described how these operations were carried out:

"Korean outlaws formed themselves into a band, four hundred strong, and, aided by Chinese bandits and Russian Bolsheviks, attacked Hunchun in September and October, 1920, during which months they set fire to and destroyed the Japanese consulate and some Japanese houses, looted valuable articles, and killed many Japanese, Koreans, and Chinese, including women and children. At the same time, refractory Koreans in North Chientao began to move, menacing the safety of Japanese and law-abiding Koreans there. Under the circumstances, the government dispatched a military expedition. . . . After a campaign of a few weeks the expedition succeeded in supressing the Korean outlaws. About five thousand of them surrendered."[3]

Even though the account is distorted, it is obvious that Korean guerrillas were a major source of annoyance to the Japanese. Their successes increased the influence of leftists within the Provisional Government, and prompted some defections. A Korean Revolutionary Party, led by Kim Won-bong, drew some leftists from the Provisional Government.

The Japanese occupation of Manchuria in 1931 brought renewed activity on the part of the government-in-exile. The Provisional Government was reorganized with Kim Koo as president, while Rhee was sent to Geneva to plead Korea's case there. In April 1932, a Korean nationalist hurled a bomb in Shanghai which killed General Shirakawa, commander of the Japanese armies in China, and wounded Mamoru Shigemitsu, later foreign minister, and Admiral Nomura, Japan's ambassador in Washington at the time of Pearl Harbor. Among those arrested in the wake of the assassination was Ahn Chang-ho, and tortures suffered while in prison hastened his death in 1938.

In Geneva, Rhee was unsuccessful in his attempts to present Korea's case before the League of Nations. His failure prompted him to try a new tactic: encouraged by the Chinese ambassador to Switzerland, Rhee applied for a visa to Moscow. With Japanese expansion posing a threat to the Soviet Union as well as to China, he hoped for a more friendly reception than he had found in the West. The Soviets, however, had so adequate a foothold among Koreans in the U.S.S.R. and Manchuria that they felt no compunction to aid that exile faction least amenable to Soviet control. In any case, the U.S.S.R. was by then more concerned with Nazi Germany than with imperial Japan.

Rhee's visit to Moscow was not unlike his unsuccessful representations elsewhere, except that it showed him willing to solicit even Communist aid on behalf of the Provisional Government. His visit to Switzerland was a turning point in his personal life, however, for there he met Francesca Donner, whom he married the following year. Rhee returned to the United States to make arrangements for Miss Donner to enter the country. He was fifty-nine and she thirty-six when they were married on October 8, 1933. It would be the lot of Francesca Rhee, the daughter of an Austrian nobleman, to become the first lady of an Asian nation which she had never seen.

The following year was largely taken up with a speaking tour of the United States. Rhee had become increasingly isolated from the Provisional Government, as a result of personality clashes, geographic separation, and the fact that the Provisional Government had its hands full with internal troubles. In 1936, however, a number of hitherto rival factions in China merged into a conservative Korean National Front with its headquarters in Hangchow, thus maintaining a semblance of unity under rightist leadership.

In 1939, with friction among Koreans in Hawaii making his church and school endeavors increasingly difficult, Rhee moved to Washington. There he took advantage of the growing popular concern over Japan to publish his own indictment of the Japanese, *Japan Inside Out*. As was to be expected, the book was a long résumé of Japanese encroachments in Korea. But in addition it contained early symptoms that Rhee had come to view himself as a Korean Moses. His description of the abortive independence movement of the 1890's left little doubt as to whom Rhee regarded as its driving force:

"The conservative Korean government, having a childlike faith in [its treaties with foreign powers] opened everything to the Japanese without preparing for national defense. It was in 1895, soon after the close of the Sino-Japanese war, that I came to realize the danger and undertook to inform the nation of the imminent danger to our national existence. I started the first daily newspaper in Korea, through the columns of which I did all I could to cause our people to know what the Japanese and the Russians, the two rival forces, were trying to do. In cooperation with many patriotic leaders, we [*sic*] succeeded in arousing a sufficient number of people to join with us in inaugurating a national defense program."[4]

Moreover, for all of Rhee's studies in international law at Harvard and Princeton, he continued to regard the old treaty of amity between the United States and Korea as a guarantee of American protection:

"If [the Korean emperor's appeal for U.S. protection against Japan] was really foolish, the Koreans were not alone responsible for it. The United States Senate and the President of the United States, as well as the State Department, all gave their approval and affixed their signatures to the treaty, thus making it a law of the United States. . . . This is, indeed, a blemish on the glorious pages of American history. Korea paid heavily for being a peace-loving nation and putting her trust in the sanctity of international treaties."[5]

Finally, although Rhee provided some documentation for his charges of a Japanese blueprint for world conquest, he offered only generalities when it came to the question of how to meet the Japanese threat. While denying that he espoused preventive war, Rhee called upon the United States to check Japan "before it is too late." But how Japan was to be checked in 1939 short of war is never made clear, and when it came to Japan's exact intentions, Rhee's crystal ball was no better than that of the average American. "The open Japanese threats of war against the United States are only a bluff," he wrote. "They know too well that it would be suicidal for them to plunge into war with the United States while Great Britain and China are menacing the Axis lineup from both ends."[6]

The concept of deterrence through preparedness was fundamental with Rhee, and his later demands as president of South Korea that the Free World unite against communism would only echo his earlier "program" to check Japan. The stalemate in the Korean War further convinced Rhee that if sufficient force could be brought to bear, his enemies would back down or quit.

Rhee's get-tough policy was suitable for situations in which the vital interests of a major power were clearly threatened. Had it been adopted by England and France in the 1930's, the rise of Hitler might have been forestalled. But in seeking allies for Korea, Rhee made no allowance for the unwillingness of any power to commit itself outside its areas of interest; indeed, he regarded the United States as having committed a breach of faith in not having protected his homeland against the Japanese. It is ironic that the threat of communism would bring about Rhee's wildest hope: that the United States become the guarantor of Korean independence.

5: The Expatriate

TO THOSE few Americans who thought at all of Korea in the frantic days following the attack on Pearl Harbor, the Hermit Kingdom was merely an early victim of Japanese aggression, a nation which would presumably be restored to freedom after the defeat of the Japanese. But to Syngman Rhee, Pearl Harbor was a dream come true. With the irrepressible optimism of the political exile, he felt certain that Pearl Harbor, by unleashing America's industrial might against the Axis powers, foreshadowed the defeat of Japan.

America's entry into the war, which shifted the center of resistance against Japan from China to the United States, bolstered Rhee's prestige within the Korean independence movement at a time when his stock had reached a low point. In 1940, a new amalgamation of factions within the Provisional Government had resulted in the formation of the Korean Independence Party, under the leadership of Kim Koo. Shortly thereafter, Kim formally supplanted Rhee as president of the Provisional Government. But now events had placed Rhee in a position more favorable than that of his rivals in Shanghai and Chungking. Korea's redemption would come not through China but from across the Pacific.

In Washington, Rhee refused to recognize his formal demotion but pressed the cause of the Provisional Government as its Washington representative. When his protestations elicited nothing more than expressions of sympathy from American officials,

Rhee condemned them as stupid, pro-Japanese, or pro-Russian. To Secretary of State Hull he wrote:

"The Provisional Government of the Republic of Korea is the sole representative of the Korean people, whether they are resident in Korea proper, Manchuria, Siberia, China or elsewhere, and regards itself, on the basis of the treaty of 1882, negotiated between the Government of Korea and the Government of the United States, not as a free movement . . . but as the only government agency of Korea in existence.[1]

Rhee's claims were, of course, unfounded. The old treaty of friendship between the United States and the Korean monarchy had nothing to do with the American choice regarding which Korean government to recognize. Though it was later demonstrated that it had considerable support within Korea, the Provisional Government had not in any sense of the word been chosen by the Korean people. Rhee's greatest obstacle, however, was that Korea itself did not enter into Allied war plans and therefore conjured up no sense of immediacy among American officialdom. In early 1942, the Pacific War Council discussed the possibility of granting some form of recognition to the Provisional Government, but decided to postpone any action until it might be more useful in arousing Korean opposition to Japan. As for regular diplomatic recognition, the U.S. position was summarized in reference to Korean participation in the post-war United Nations conference.

"The United Nations which are represented at the United Nations Conference on International Organization all have legally constituted governing authorities whereas the 'Korean Provisional Government' and other Korean organizations do not possess at the present time the qualities requisite for obtaining recognition by the United States as a governing authority. The 'Korean Provisional Government' has never exercised administrative authority over any part of Korea, nor can it be regarded as representative of the Korean people of today. Due to geographical and other factors its following even among exiled Koreans is inevitably limited. It is the policy of this Government in dealing with groups such as the 'Korean Provisional Government' to avoid taking action which might, when the victory of the United Nations is achieved, tend to compromise the right of the Korean people to choose the ultimate form and personnel of the government which they may wish to establish."[2]

An area in which Rhee enjoyed some success, however, was that of gaining recognition of Korean nationality apart from the Japanese citizenship that had been forced upon the Koreans. Through Attorney-General Biddle and Secretary of War Stimson, he pressed for exemption of Koreans in the United States from alien restrictions such as those requiring identification certificates and prohibiting the possession of cameras. The attorney-general issued an order to this effect, and Secretary Stimson acknowledged that he was "fully appreciative of the feelings of the many loyal Koreans now resident in this country who have never been in sympathy with the government imposed upon their homeland by military conquest."[3]

Partly as a result of the Anglo-American policy of giving priority to the defeat of Germany rather than Japan, it was not until the Cairo conference of November 1943 that Allied war aims concerning Korea were spelled out. The communiqué—framed by Roosevelt, Churchill, and Chiang Kai-shek—stated that "the aforesaid three great powers, mindful of the enslavement of the people of Korea, are determined that in due course Korea shall become free and independent." Stalin gave the communiqué his blessing at Teheran.

Among restless Koreans, the expression "in due course" brought a mixed reaction. From Chungking, Kim Koo denounced the phrase as "absurd," and demanded independence "the moment the Japanese collapse." Rhee was equally disturbed. But in Korea, where the qualifying phrase could be interpreted as meaning "shortly," the attitude was one of jubilation.[4]

American policy, reflected in the "due course" provision, was conditioned by Roosevelt's belief in the gradual introduction of self-rule into colonial areas lacking experience in self-government. In 1942 he commented:

"I like to think that the history of the Philippines in the last forty-four years provides in a very real sense a pattern for the future of other small nations and peoples of the world. . . . But . . . we must remember that such a pattern is based on two important factors. The first is that there be a period of preparation through the dissemination of education and the recognition and fulfillment of physical and social and economic needs. The second is that there be a period of training for ultimate independent sovereignty, through the practice of more and more self-government, beginning with local government and passing on through the various steps to complete statehood."[5]

This thinking prompted Roosevelt to suggest to Cordell Hull "that Manchuria and Formosa be returned to China and that Korea might be placed under an international trusteeship, with China, the United States, and one or two other countries participating."[6]

Although Roosevelt's failure to cite Russia specifically suggested an unawareness of that country's historic interest in Korea, due allowance was made at Yalta, where the proposal agreed to by Stalin provided for a trusteeship among Britain, Russia, China, and the United States. Nonetheless, the Soviets appeared cool to the prospect of a trusteeship. Averell Harriman quotes the Soviet leader as having asked why there was any need for trusteeship if the Koreans could produce a satisfactory government of their own —which Harriman concluded meant a Communist government. Roosevelt replied that the only experience the United States had in such matters was in the Philippines, where it had taken the people about fifty years to prepare for self-government. He felt that in the case of Korea the period might be twenty to thirty years. Stalin replied that the shorter the period the better, and inquired as to whether any foreign troops would be stationed in Korea. When the president replied in the negative, Stalin expressed his approval.[7]

6. Syngman Rhee (standing, fifth from right) and Mrs. Rhee (at Rhee's right) with members of the Foreign Affairs Department of the Korean Provisional Government in Washington, May 28, 1944. This photograph dates from the period when Rhee was pressing for formal recognition of the Korean Provisional Government and for a guarantee of Korea's independence at the end of World War II. (*Pacific Stars and Stripes Photo*)

The communiqué issued after the Yalta conference mentioned neither Korea nor the main purpose of the meeting, the obtaining of Soviet agreement to enter the war against Japan. But Rhee, convinced that his country had been sacrificed on the altar of Soviet intervention, leaped to the attack. In a press conference he charged a "deal" at Yalta aimed at turning Korea over to the Soviets. Repetition of his charges, which brought a denial from the State Department and then from the White House, further discredited Rhee in the eyes of American officials. These disclaimers, however, merely reinforced Rhee's belief in the existence of a conspiracy against Korea. To friends he wrote:

"In view of the anxiety in some quarters to get Russia into the Asiatic War, recognition [of the Provisional Government] may have been withheld pending a clearer formulation of Russia's desires in regard to Korea. If this were a factor, it represented either a crass willingness to trade the independence of a small nation for the support of a large one, or a timid fear of developing any foreign policy until we were able to ascertain that it would please a powerful ally. Either motive would be one we should not expect to be avowed."[8]

In the eight months between the Yalta conference and Rhee's return to Korea, great and calamitous events marked the end of World War II and the early stages of the cold war between the Communist and Free World blocs. In April 1945, Franklin Roosevelt, who had personally dominated American foreign policy during the war years, died; May brought the surrender of Germany and the long-awaited victory in Europe; in August, Japan felt the weight of the first atomic bomb.

The United States was unprepared for V-J Day. In the confusion which followed Japan's surrender, Korea was one of many problems for Pentagon planners attempting to formulate a plan for the surrender of Japanese troops. No one had foreseen the speedy capitulation of the Japanese, and the new Truman administration was still being briefed on the details of Roosevelt's personal diplomacy.

Gradually, however, the occupation of Korea loomed as a race between the Russians and the Americans. On August 12, Soviet troops began moving into North Korea. From Moscow, Ambassador Harriman and reparations representative Edwin W. Pauley, citing evidence of growing Soviet intransigence, urged that the United States occupy of as much of Korea and Manchuria as possible. On August 15, General Order No. 1, cabled to General MacArthur in Tokyo, directed U.S. forces to accept the surrender of Japanese forces in Korea south of the thirty-eighth parallel. The Soviets made no comment.[9]

Carl Berger writes: "The sad truth was that Korea was the only important area occupied by American troops in the Pacific for which detailed, concrete preparation had not been made by any branch of the United States Government."[10] Syngman Rhee, however, had waited years for this day. At an age when most men had long retired, Rhee fought State Department red tape in an attempt to return to Korea ahead of his Shanghai rivals. For him, the day of deliverance was at hand.

His exile over, Rhee nevertheless found himself in an anomalous position with respect to his own role in Korean politics. On one hand, years of agitation on behalf of Korean independence had made his name nearly a legend even in Korea itself. In addition, he spoke the language and knew the ways of Korea's liberators—a considerable advantage considering the provinciality of his rivals.

On the other hand, even in the Orient, Rhee's advanced age was a handicap to his political prospects. He was no longer president of the Provisional Government, and he faced younger and powerful rivals in Kim Koo and Kim Kyu-sic. In North Korea an ominous note was the publicity being accorded by the Soviets to an obscure guerrilla leader, Kim Il-sung. Finally, Rhee was not exactly a favorite of the Americans. Years of sniping at the State Department had had an effect, and when the American army entered Korea it was hardly to set Syngman Rhee up as president.

As for Rhee himself, four decades of life in the United States had neither mellowed his outlook nor broadened his perspective beyond the borders of Korea. Never an original thinker, in his old age Rhee tended increasingly to follow set channels of thinking: hatred of the Japanese, fear of the Soviets, and a driving ambition to go down in history as the first president of a united Korean republic. By 1945, he had come to regard himself as the embodiment of the new Korea, a Moses who had led his people out of the wilderness.

The Syngman Rhee who returned to Korea after World War II was a strange mixture of Western idealism and Oriental guile. He believed in collective security with a Wilsonian fervor, and viewed the American occupation of South Korea as a fortuitous guarantee of American interest in Korea. He wanted Korea to be set up as a democratic republic, but only if he could be chief executive and his power could be supreme. To protect his position and increase his power he was prepared to make use of every means available. Rhee's dealings with Korean exiles in Hawaii, however discordant, had been educational. In Honolulu there were a church and a school to testify that when Rhee could not destroy his rivals he could still forge his own way.

Divided in half by foreign occupation, and projected overnight into the stuggle between Communist and Free World blocs, "liberated" Korea seemed hardly better off than under the Japanese. And from all sides came ambitious political exiles, anxious to fill and exploit what political vacuum might exist under the aegis of the occupying powers.

6: Divided Korea

WHEN THE plane bearing Syngman Rhee from Tokyo touched down at Kimpo Airfield on October 16, 1945, the American occupation of Korea was scarcely five weeks old. Nevertheless, even this short period had brought hints of the political complexities which would make the former Hermit Kingdom one of the most difficult problems with which the United States found herself saddled at the end of World War II. Already there were the first manifestations of the Soviet intransigence which would make Korea one of the sore spots of the cold war. And already there were strained relations between the occupying American army and the Korean populace, with the military authorities at odds with a *de facto* Korean government which had met them on arrival.

On September 8—nearly a month after the first units of Soviet troops entered North Korea—U.S. Army units of Lieutenant General John R. Hodge's 24th Corps had landed at Inchon. For a week previous, American B-29's had dropped leaflets informing the Korean populace of the imminent arrival of American troops. If the Americans had fears of latent Japanese resistance, they were groundless; Japanese troops had initially resisted the Soviet advance across the Yalu, but those in the south were relieved to be surrendering to the Americans instead of the Russians. In the north, some Japanese joined an increasing trickle of Korean refugees moving south as reports of Soviet depredations spread.

To educated Koreans, the surrender of Japan came as no surprise. Neither did it surprise the Japanese governor-general, Nobuyuki Abe. In early August, Abe had approached several known Korean nationalists concerning the formation of an interim Korean government prior to the Japanese surrender as a means of maintaining order and forestalling reprisals against the Japanese. Finally he proposed to Lyuh Wun-hyung, a moderate leftist with a considerable local following, that he accept governing authority until the arrival of the Americans.

Lyuh was Korea's handsomest politician, a ringing orator whose delivery had won him as many adherents as had his agrarian socialist philosophy. Lyuh's followers, however, were not entirely pleased when he accepted Abe's proposal. Some were adherents of the Provisional Government who feared that Lyuh's self-proclaimed "People's Republic" would impugn the legitimacy of the Shanghai government. Others feared that any collaboration with the Japanese would damage Lyuh's stature as a resistance leader. Under the Japanese, Lyuh had supported the Provisional Government; now, with almost a free hand in Korea, he vacillated between his previous commitments and the temptation to strike out on his own.

In an arrangement unique in Korean history, Lyuh and his People's Republic administered the government of Korea from August 15 to September 8, 1945. They were largely successful in preventing violence, and developed considerable grass roots support through the formation of People's Committees in the countryside. In a further attempt to generate popular support, Lyuh called for land reforms which would enable peasants to purchase land on easy terms, the ouster of Japanese nationals and Korean collaborators from positions of authority, expansion of the suffrage, of the formation of agricultural cooperatives, and strict regulation of government monopolies.[1]

When General Hodge arrived in Inchon, he was met by officials of the People's Republic representing themselves as a legal government of Korea. Hopefully, they looked to the Americans for some sign of accommodation, but there was none. Hodge knew nothing of Lyuh or his government, and its choice of the name "People's Republic" was hardly fortuitous. When MacArthur in Tokyo supported Hodge with a statement that Korea would be ruled under his authority, the People's Republic was out in the cold. Ignoring Lyuh, Hodge announced that Abe and other Japanese officials would be retained in office temporarily to facilitate the inauguration of military government.

Here, however, Hodge had touched on a sensitive point with all Koreans. The popular reaction to his pronouncement was one of indignation. Had Korea been "liberated" only to remain under Japanese rule? The outcry was so great that Hodge hastily rescinded his order, but not before the prestige of the occupation had been dealt a severe blow and the Lyuh organization set firmly in opposition to the military government.

Lyuh did not take his setback quietly. With reports from his People's Committees reflecting continued support for the People's Republic, Lyuh and his cohorts launched an attack against the military government. Demonstrations were staged in the cities, and anti-American posters and pamphlets were given wide distribution. Lyuh's attacks on the occupation, together with the fact that he spoke less frequently of his loyalty to the Provisional Government, encouraged a belief among the Americans that the People's Republic was Communist-dominated and that Lyuh was an opportunist attempting to seize the reins of government.

Meanwhile, relations between the Americans and the Soviet authorities in North Korea were no more satisfactory. Economic conditions in the south worsened as a result of the sudden partitioning of the Korean peninsula, which separated the industrial north from the agrarian south. In addition, the Soviets controlled the supply of electric power to the south and were prone to cut off the flow from time to time to remind the Americans that they were there. General Hodge, however, was repeatedly rebuffed in his efforts to contact his Soviet counterpart. Faced with the Russians in the north and the People's Republic in the south, Hodge labored to bring a degree of political stability to South Korea.

When Rhee arrived in Seoul in October, any doubts about his personal popularity were quickly put to rest. The warmth of his welcome stemmed in part from his being the first of Korea's exile leaders to return, but there was no questioning its fervor. Crowds cheered Rhee from outside a suite in the Chosun Hotel which, interestingly, had been reserved for him by General Hodge. Rhee was moved to write:

"It seems the whole nation is agog since my arrival was announced. Hundreds of people gather around the hotel entrance and ask for a chance to see me. General Hodge and I had agreed not to announce my arrival until we are [*sic*] ready but the next morning the general came and said the American news reporters were demanding an interview. So we rushed to the Palace and entered the press conference, with General Hodge and General Arnold escorting me. Then I spoke both in English and Korean. Since that time to this, crowds gathered in front of the outside gate and many men and women managed to come inside and I could not find one minute for rest. Yesterday afternoon I had to call to them, saying they must go away and do their work."[2]

Coming as he did in the wake of General Hodge's brush with the People's Republic, Rhee found himself considerably more welcome to the U.S. Army in Korea than to the State Department in Washington. His popularity and known conservatism made him appear at minimum a useful counterpoise to Lyuh Wun-hung and, at best, a friendly interpreter of occupation policies to the Korean populace. In practice, it proved nearly impossible to work with Rhee. He had waited long for his return, and the cheering crowd was heady wine. Making good use of his personal popularity, Rhee moved swiftly to set up his own organization. Insisting that he himself was above partisan politics, Rhee called upon all political groups to join in a Central Committee for the Rapid Realization of Independence, an action which served to identify him personally with the national aspiration which had been

7. Syngman Rhee (front center) with members of the Korean delegation to the United Nations Conference, San Francisco, May, 1945. Rhee's failure to gain formal recognition for the Korean Provisional Government resulted in Korea's exclusion as a member nation at the conference. (*Pacific Stars and Stripes Photo*)

somewhat dashed by General Hodge's pronouncements. Even the Communists joined the C.C.R.R.I. for a time.

When Kim Koo, Kim Kyu-sic, and other members of the Provisional Government arrived in Seoul in November, they found their erstwhile Washington representative the acknowledged leader of the conservative independence forces, and enjoying the tacit blessing of the American authorities. Although the Provisional Government, too, returned to a popular welcome, it was nonetheless apparent that Rhee had stolen a march on them on the South Korean political scene.

By December 1945, the American-Soviet impasse over Korea was complete. With the northern half of the peninsula having fallen behind the iron curtain, establishment of an independent, united Korea was an impossibility. Although U.S. authorities in Seoul acknowledged the popular desire for independence, the State Department felt it had no alternative other than to proceed with previous plans for the establishment of a trusteeship. Secretary Byrnes, however, advised Hodge that if adequate guarantees of Korea's unification and independence could be obtained from the Soviets, it might be possible for the United States to discontinue its support of trusteeship.[3]

At the Moscow conference which began on December 16, however, the American delegation called for a four-power trusteeship and the establishment of a U.S.—Soviet Joint Commission to settle administrative problems arising from the occupation. The Soviets agreed, proposing in addition that measures be taken leading to an interim government, to which the United States agreed.

When news of the Moscow agreement reached Korea on December 28, the reaction was violent. All parties opposed trusteeship, but the conservative groups were particularly vocal. Rhee and Kim Koo organized demonstrations, and Kim established an Anti-Trusteeship Committee which called a general strike by all government authorities. Kim, who had hitherto sidestepped the question of the legal status of the Provisional Government out of deference to General Hodge, now ordered that the police take orders only from him.

For three days crowds milled in the streets of Seoul. Then, on New Year's day, the Communists received word not to oppose trusteeship. Signs which had read "Down with Trusteeship" were hastily changed to read "Up with Trusteeship." Moscow's unrealistic order that the Korean Communists support the Moscow declaration cost the party dearly in terms of popular support, and permitted Rhee and Kim Koo to turn the anti-trusteeship demonstrations into a display of solidarity by the rightists.

Although the trusteeship debacle went far to discredit the Communists, the rightists still did not have the field to themselves. On January 3, 1946, a correspondent for the *Christian Science Monitor* wrote that "the so-called People's Republic, composed of Socialist and Communist elements, enjoys far more popular support than any other single political grouping."[4] It was difficult to determine trends, however, for party lines were blurred. Every shade of political thought was represented in minor parties and personal followings which mushroomed in every province. By June 1946, there were no less than 107 registered parties in South Korea!

As the Communists and the conservatives clashed over the trusteeship issue, the most striking characteristic of the Korean political scene was the absence of strong center groups. The closest thing to a third force was the Democratic Party of Song Chinwoo, whose platform of a government-regulated economy and a welfare state was not radical for Korea. Song was assassinated in December 1945, however, and his popular following, never great, was largely limited to the southern provinces.

By the spring of 1946, the military government had all but backed into a position of supporting Syngman Rhee. He was outspoken in his denunciations of the Communists while—at a time when memories of the general strike were still fresh—seemingly more responsible than Kim Koo. His followers were making increasing use of strong-arm methods, but in conversations with

Americans Rhee stressed his devotion to democratic principles. If Rhee was somewhat less than sympathetic with the military government, it was hoped that he could be reasoned with. Besides, who else was there?

On the international scene, spring brought the first attempt to break the Korean stalemate under the provisions of the Moscow accord. On March 20, the Joint Soviet-American Commission convened in Seoul to discuss a provisional government. It became quickly apparent, however, that the Soviets were not interested in cooperation. The Communists insisted that anyone who had ever expressed criticism of trusteeship should be ineligible for consultation in connection with the proposed provisional government—action which would exclude virtually all rightist spokesmen, including Rhee. When the United States balked at any such broad exclusions, the talks adjourned *sine die* on May 20.

The cold-war chill cast its blight on the Korean spring. When the Russians denied the United States the right to maintain consular representation in Pyongyang, the Russian consular staff was forced in turn to withdraw from Seoul. The division of Korea was complete. Although Hodge forwarded to his Soviet counterpart several proposals for reconvening the Joint Commission, there was a growing feeling that if anything was to be accomplished, it would have to be on a higher level.

Meanwhile, Syngman Rhee was laying the groundwork for his own political rise. The return of Kim Koo in November had forced him to share the political spotlight, and the sequence of events at the turn of the year had forced Rhee to stay close to Seoul. In mid-February, however, Rhee embarked on a month's speaking tour of southern Korea.

Rhee stumped the provinces, stressing the twin themes of independence and unification. He was acutely aware that he lacked organizational backing such as Lyuh Wun-hyung enjoyed from the People's Republic and Kim Koo from the Provisional Government. Anticipating a showdown, Rhee determined to make maximum use of his popular reputation as the basis of a new party.

His speaking tour, which he felt to be in the true Wilsonian tradition, served the dual purpose of solidifying his grass-roots support and laying the groundwork for an organization of his own which would eventually eclipse those of all his rivals.

Although ill for two weeks in March, Rhee returned to his task in May. Continuing to maintain that he was himself above politics, he plumped for the National Society for the Rapid Realization of Independence, an enlarged version of the earlier C.C.R.R.I. but still dominated by Rhee's followers. The right, led by the National Society, began to gain ground at the expense of the People's Republic, but these same gains left Lyuh's organization vulnerable to the Communists.

Rhee might have strengthened the non-Communist bloc, and isolated the Communists in their unpopular anti-trusteeship stand, by an offer of compromise to the hard-pressed People's Republic. But he doubtless had an inkling that Korean unification was not to be readily achieved and that in time a separate South Korean government would be the only feasible way of achieving self-government in the south. To this end Rhee continued to demand unification while simultaneously seeking to consolidate his control of the right without any dilution by leftist elements less responsive to his leadership. To Rhee it was difficult enough to have to head the National Society with Kim Koo and Kim Kyu-sic as vice-chairmen.

In the remainder of 1946, Rhee's prestige continued to increase. His followers inaugurated a campaign to develop a loyal following among the police. Businessmen anxious for a conservative government provided financial support. Fence-sitters who were anti-Communist but not necessarily pro-Rhee were told that he was the political favorite of the Americans.

Spurned by Rhee, Lyuh Wun-hyung debated some form of coalition with the moderate rightists of Kim Kyu-sic. But the Communists, who hoped to dominate the center as well as the left, feared any centrist alliance which might develop between Lyuh and Kim. The negotiations came to an abrupt halt in July when Lyuh was assassinated, presumably by the Communists, while driving through the streets of Seoul.

If the Communists were losing ground in South Korea, they were nonetheless flourishing in the north. Although a trickle of refugees continued to find its way south, a massive land reform in March 1946 went far towards erasing memories of the initial Soviet occupation in North Korea. According to a decree issued by the Soviet-sponsored People's Committees, all land not personally tilled, together with all land in excess of 12½ acres, was to be turned over to the People's Committees for distribution to the landless. In October, all Japanese assets—mines, factories, and warehouses—were confiscated and nationalized in the name of the People's Committees.

The Soviets' next move was to provide a degree of legitimacy for a puppet regime in the north, and the summer of 1946 brought preparations for elections to be held in the fall. Significantly, the People's Committees accorded full propaganda treatment to one Kim Song-ju, until then an obscure guerrilla captain in Manchuria, who had assumed the name of a far more renowned partisan leader, Kim Il-sung. Meanwhile, the People's Committees gave way to a National Democratic Front which, although tightly controlled by the Communists, included several minor parties and provided a useful democratic façade.

When elections for various levels of People's Committees were held on November 3, 1946, the National Democratic Front received ninety-seven per cent of the vote cast. In the wake of this sweeping endorsement the Communists convened a constituent assembly for the purpose of forming an interim government. To the surprise of no one, Kim Il-sung emerged as premier. At no time was the Communist takeover seriously challenged; dissenters found it easier to go south than to face Soviet bayonets. The founding of the Pyongyang regime stands as a model for the establishment of satellite nations, accomplished under the optimum conditions of Soviet military occupation. Key positions, such as those dealing with the police and the military, were quickly filled with Koreans who had lived in or been trained in the U.S.S.R.

Even while consolidating their grip in the north, however, the Communists watched their prospects in South Korea deteriorate. The South Korean Labor Party of Pak Hun-young was proving unable to check the drift to the right, partly because of the efforts of Rhee and others but in large measure as a result of the pro-trusteeship albatross hung about its neck by Moscow. In desperation, Park's 20,000-man following turned to violence.

The Korean Communists had all along used violent means for specific ends and to counter intimidation by the rightists. Now they attempted to undermine political stability in South Korea through riots and strikes. In the industrial city of Taegu the Communists began a campaign of agitation and vilification against the police, whose cruelty under the Japanese made them vulnerable to popular anger, and whose support of the right made them a threat to the Communists. In the riots which ensued, fifty-nine policemen were killed by Communist-instigated mobs, most by being sprayed with gasoline and burned. North Kyongsang province was placed under martial law by the military government, and the riots were finally quelled by a thousand police brought in from Seoul. Sporadic outbreaks continued until mid-October, however, when most of the agitators escaped to the countryside.

The Taegu riots showed what the Communists could do in stirring up unrest in the south, but over the long term they were probably counterproductive. Although out of consideration for Soviet sensibilities the Labor Party was not outlawed immediately, tightened security measures nevertheless drove the party underground. And as time went on, the Communist terror campaign was recognized as a virtual admission of the party's inability to achieve its objectives by non-violent means.

To American officials, the riots served as a vivid reminder of the powder keg on which they were sitting, and prompted the military government to intensify its efforts to develop political cohesion among non-Communist groups. But to those Koreans who chose to listen to Radio Pyongyang, there was a superficial contrast in the fact that whereas North Korea was moving towards at least nominal government by Koreans, the United States appeared to be making only grudging concessions towards self-government in the south.

Any attempt to unify non-Communist groups, however, would have to reckon with Syngman Rhee. In a year's time Rhee had relegated Lyuh Wun-hyung to the sidelines, and taken over leadership of the scores of personal factions, organizations, and cliques which, taken together, constituted the political right. With the National Society now providing Rhee with his own organizational backing, and with growing support at the grass roots and among the police, Rhee was in no mood to "compromise" with the potpourri of Korean politicos to whom General Hodge now turned.

7: Half a Loaf

SELDOM has a military occupation faced as trying a situation as that which confronted General Hodge in 1946. In the first place, the Koreans argued that theirs was not a conquered country, and that there was no justification for ruling by military government. Yet the prospect of turning over the government to any of South Korea's leading political groupings was scarcely inviting. The extreme right and extreme left appeared quite capable of initiating civil war over the issues of separate elections and trusteeship, while there seemed to be no moderates in Korean politics. Unable to promise the South Koreans self-rule, Hodge sought to foster political stability as best he could.

A number of factors, however, tended to encourage political extremism and inhibit the development of center parties in the south. First, there was the question of unification, which forced one to choose between the alternatives of negotiating with the Communists or of accepting the fact of a divided Korea. Second, there was the fact that Korea's most effective political leaders—with Rhee a case in point—tended to represent the extremes. Moderates like Lyuh Wun-hyung and Kim Kyu-sic found it extremely difficult to come up with workable "compromise" solutions to the unification impasse. Finally, the emotional issues of the day underscored the historical Korean penchant for disputation and discord, and discouraged efforts at compromise among major political groups.

While Korea's fate was still uncertain, Hodge moved in late

1946 to increase Korean participation in governmental administration. The following year brought establishment of the South Korean Interim Government (S.K.I.G.), under which a large sector of the occupation administration was turned over to the Koreans. While S.K.I.G. helped remove some of the onus of occupation, such "Koreanization" measures had little effect in improving Hodge's relations with the local politicos where policy considerations were concerned. When Hodge named Rhee as the head of a rightist-dominated advisory group called the Democratic Council, the new body spent most of its time composing resolutions attacking the military government.

While Rhee by this time was no longer the fair-haired boy of the Americans, almost all of Hodge's moves to increase Korean participation in government served to strengthen Rhee's hand. When Hodge proposed the establishment of an interim legislative assembly, to be filled half by appointment and half by indirect elections, he triggered a major struggle for power in South Korea. Rightist groups interpreted the move as a step in the direction of South Korean independence as espoused by Rhee. Leftist groups attacked the proposed assembly as an American move to perpetuate the division of Korea.

Rhee's ability to make political capital out of occupation policy, together with Communist blunders such as their espousal of trusteeship, strengthened the position of the right for the elections to the Interim Assembly held in November 1946. So did organizational strides by the National Society, which was able to gain the support of a large segment of the provincial police following the Taegu riots. But the extent of the rightist victory—rightist candidates carried forty-three out of forty-five elected seats—came as a surprise. When Kim Kyu-sic and Lyuh Wun-hyung complained loudly of rightist terrorism, Hodge became convinced that the election had not represented the popular will, and he favored the moderates in his own appointments to the assembly. Hodge's action infuriated Rhee and Kim Koo, and Kim for a time considered proclaiming the legitimacy of the old Provisional Government in the hope that popular sentiment would rally to him. Rhee, however, had other plans; in true Wilsonian fashion, he would carry his case to the American people.

By the spring of 1947, the question of independence had become a crucial one in South Korea. Rhee, who would later become the great spokesman for unification, came increasingly to favor separate elections in the south and the withdrawal of U.S. military forces from Korea. Rhee's motives were a subject of controversy even at the time; his admirers depicted Rhee as recognizing that one cannot negotiate in good faith with Communists, while his detractors insisted that Rhee could never be elected president unless the elections were held under U.S. auspices and he could claim U.S. support.

Rhee did not leave for America without providing for a vigorous rear-guard action. In the Interim Assembly his supporters demanded separate elections in long orations which effectively blocked efforts by some members to deal with more prosaic matters such as the ruinous economic difficulties besetting the country. So widespread were the rumors of separate elections that Hodge was compelled to announce:

"Either through lack of knowledge of fact or through malicious intent to deceive the Korean people, certain elements are creating the impression that the United States now favors and is actively working towards a separate government in southern Korea. . . . [Such] assumptions are incorrect and dangerous conclusions, entirely without justification, and are contrary to the announced basic policies of the United States."[1]

In Washington, Rhee attacked Hodge for his appointments to the Interim Assembly, and attempted to disparage the opposition of Kim Koo and Kim Kyu-sic to separate elections in the south. His press statements, bristling with references to democracy and the people's will, had much of the appeal of a Fourth of July oration. Some of the impact was lost, however, because of Rhee's invective against the occupation. On January 23, Rhee charged Hodge with favoring Korean leftists and with "building up and fostering the Korean Communist Party."[2] Rhee justified his own opposition to the occupation by charging that Hodge was an autocrat and a tool of the Communists.

Had Rhee shown a little patience with the military government, Soviet intransigence would have eventually dictated the need for separate elections such as Rhee espoused. Instead, Rhee was now handicapped by his reputation as a trouble maker. American officials weighed his unquestionable popularity in Korea against his stubbornness, his penchant for distorting and discrediting American policies, and the trend toward strong-arm methods by his supporters in Korea. Rhee drew noncommittal replies in his demands for South Korean elections, but found the Pentagon delighted with any prospect of an American military withdrawal from Korea.

Meanwhile, with Rhee's followers in Korea growing restless, and with Kim Koo still threatening to set up his Provisional Government, it became inadvisable for Rhee to prolong his stay in the United States. Having decided to return to Korea, he announced in a press conference that the State Department had agreed to hold separate elections in South Korea at an early date. Rhee's announcement, presumably designed to enhance his prestige at home, brought a denial from the State Department.[3] But denials often do not catch up with the original claim, and in Korea there were many who believed that where there was smoke there was fire.

The diplomatic impasse over Korea continued until the spring of 1947. In May, however, an exchange of notes between the State Department and the Soviet Foreign Office brought about a reconvening of the Joint Commission in Seoul.

At first the new negotiations went smoothly. By agreeing that Koreans who actively opposed the Moscow decision should not be consulted by the Allied Powers, the United States showed itself willing to sacrifice Rhee and his cohorts on the altar of negotiated unification. In return, the Communists agreed to accept for consultation a number of political groups which had previously opposed trusteeship but which were now prepared to abide by the Moscow accord. The reconvening of the Joint Commission was a measure of the unhappy fate befalling Korea, in that unification if achieved at all would probably come in the form of trusteeship.

When the Joint Commission met on May 22, it immediately became the target of sniping by the rightists and their front groups. On his return from America, Rhee revived his Anti-Trusteeship Committee and staged mass demonstrations during sessions of the Joint Commission. Although the American negotiators were embarrassed by Rhee's activities, which were cited by the Communists as U.S. provocations designed to disrupt the conference, it was ultimately the Soviets who brought about the breakdown of the conference. The American attitude in the cold war was gradually stiffening: March brought the first announcement of U.S. aid to Greece and Turkey, and June brought enunciation of the Marshall Plan. In Seoul, early July saw the Soviets revert to their old position of opposing consultation with anyone who had ever expressed opposition to the Moscow agreement. The lines of the cold war now extended from Athens to Seoul.

The Joint Commission continued to meet through the summer and fall of 1947, but the U.S. attitude toward it underwent a metamorphosis. A ban on demonstrations against the commission was relaxed, and South Korean Communists were periodically rounded up by U.S. authorities. Violence flared in July, as rightist "youth groups" and terrorists joined the police in searching out subversive elements. It came to a head on July 19 with the assassination of Lyuh Wun-hyung, who had been discussing with Kim Kyu-sic the formation of a center party. Since both the Communists and the rightists had reason to oppose a centrist coalition, the ultimate responsibility for Lyuh's assassination remains unclear to this day.

On September 17, in a momentous step, the United States placed the Korean problem before the United Nations. This action was the first of a series of skillful moves in which the United States abdicated sole responsibility for South Korea, and indirectly laid the groundwork for later U.N. participation in the Korean War. The Soviet response was an attempt to regain the propaganda initiative. In the Joint Commission, the Soviets proposed that all foreign troops withdraw from Korea during 1948, leaving the Koreans free to establish their own government. For all the superficial appeal of the Communist proposal, the United States now found it unacceptable. Information reaching the Pentagon indicated that the Soviets were engaged in a major military buildup in North Korea, and as early as February 1947, Hodge had advised President Truman that Rhee's claim that the North Koreans were equipping a 500,000-man army appeared correct.[4]

In November 1947, a Soviet-sponsored resolution calling for a joint troop withdrawal from Korea so that Korea might set up a government "without foreign intervention" was voted down in the United Nations Assembly. Instead, the assembly adopted an American resolution calling for a Temporary Commission on Korea which could "travel, observe, and consult throughout Korea," and which would observe the election of a Korean national assembly to be held no later than March 31, 1948. Significantly, both the American and Soviet resolutions anticipated Korean independence at an early date. The spectre of an unwanted trusteeship was finally laid to rest.

The implications of U.N.-supervised elections had repercussions all over Korea. When the U.N. Commission arrived in Korea it was, to no one's surprise, snubbed by the Russians, who refused it entry into North Korea. Opposition to elections in South Korea alone, however, was widespread. In consultation with the U.N. Commission, Kim Kyu-sic admitted that he knew of no simple solution to the Korean dilemma, but stated that he opposed separate elections on the grounds that they would formalize the division of Korea. Kim Koo also opposed separate elections, and proposed a joint troop withdrawal from Korea with the United Nations taking over responsibility for maintaining order.

Rhee, on his part, demanded separate elections, while now

calling for the retention of U.S. troops in South Korea until large security forces could be trained. Insisting that South Korea would have been self-governing long ago except for Hodge's opposition, Rhee charged the American commander once again with fostering the growth of Korean communism, and threatened that should the United States fail to permit elections "the people" would carry them out anyhow.*

It soon became apparent that Rhee, the early apostle of separate elections, had gambled and won. While strategic and military considerations rather than Rhee's polemics had led the United States to place the Korean issue before the United Nations, the result was what Rhee desired. Within the U.N. Commission there were sharp differences as to the advisability of separate elections, but its eventual recommendation was in favor of elections as in accordance with the general Korean desire for independence.

Those who opposed the commission's decision did not give up without a final effort. In April, North Korea sponsored a unity conference in Pyongyang, ostensibly to promote unification but in fact to delay the South Korean elections which had been scheduled for May. Both Kim Koo and Kim Kyu-sic attended from the South. The conference was inconclusive—as the Communists doubtless planned that it should be—and Kim Koo later denounced them for their insincerity. Kim Kyu-sic, however, returned to repeat Communist assurances of their fraternal regard for the South Koreans, assurances which took on a hollow ring as North Korea continued its harassing raids across the thirty-eighth parallel and initiated periodic cutoffs of South Korea's electric power supply.

The elections of May 10, 1948, were hardly held in an ideal atmosphere. Communist-inspired riots in February had brought

* *New York Times*, January 28, 1948. The *New York Times* correspondent in Seoul, Richard J. H. Johnston, wrote on January 31 that "the 68-year-old Dr. Kim [Kyu-sic] emerged this week as the outstanding moderate in the eyes of the United Nations Commission," but described Kim's lack of organizational support and his distaste for partisan politics as political liabilities.

at least thirty-seven deaths and more than eight thousand arrests, and had created an air of suspicion and suppression which the commission viewed with extreme concern. Widespread doubts were expressed as to the wisdom of holding elections at all, and as to whether the political maturity of the Koreans was sufficient to make elections a valid expression of the popular will. The situation was further complicated by the fact that the elections were being boycotted by the followers of Kim Koo and Kim Kyu-sic.

Although the Assembly to be elected was to choose a president—presumably from its own number—Rhee himself put on an initial show of not running for the Assembly. Only at the eleventh hour, upon the entreaty of friends, did Rhee allow his name to be registered in a Seoul district. His nominating petition duly received more than forty thousand signatures—many times more than the two hundred required for registration.

One of Rhee's peculiarities was that, not satisfied with his very genuine political popularity, he went to great pains to create the illusion that he was above politics, beyond challenge, and served only at the demand of the people. Now, after Rhee had with seeming reluctance put his hat in the ring, his followers made every effort to insure that he ran unopposed in his district. When a political unknown, one Choi Neung-chin, attempted to circulate his own nominating petition, pro-Rhee toughs successfully discouraged the citizenry from signing his petition.

When the votes were tallied, the result showed that despite the boycott about 72 per cent of the eligible voters went to the polls. Although no party gained a clear majority, Rhee's National Society for the Rapid Realization of Independence led with 55 seats, with Kim Sung-soo's conservative Korean Democratic Party next with 28 seats. Two right-wing groups, the Taedong Youth Corps and the Racial Youth Corps, won 12 and 6 seats respectively. Representatives of minor parties and 85 independents—many of whom were rightist-inclined—rounded out the 198-man Assembly. The conservative complexion of the new Assembly stemmed from

8. Syngman Rhee and General Douglas MacArthur at the ceremonies held in Seoul, August 15, 1948, for the proclamation of the new Republic of Korea. On this occasion, governing authority was transferred to the new R.O.K. government. (*Photo by courtesy of Horace Bristol*)

several factors: the boycott by the leftists and Kim Koo, the successful use of strong-arm tactics by the Rhee group, and the essential conservatism of Korea, as well as the obvious fact of Rhee's personal popularity. There were numerous instances of intimidation, though not so many as feared by the U.N. Commission. As a test of sentiment, however, the elections were at best a qualified success. The Koreans were almost totally without experience in self-government, and in many areas the farmers merely requested the village elders to instruct them how to vote.

When the Assembly convened for the first time on May 31, it recognized Rhee as the person most responsible for its existence by electing him chairman—a first step to the presidency. It then turned to the drafting of a constitution. Then as afterwards, there was sentiment both for a strong executive modeled after that of the United States, and for a parliamentary government in which the cabinet would be responsible to the Assembly. The document finally adopted on July 17 provided for a president elected by the Assembly but enjoying strong independent powers. His choice of prime minister had to be approved by the Assembly, but that of other ministers did not. Both the president and the Assembly were to serve terms of four years.

While displaying some of the trappings of parliamentary government, the constitution left the door open for a strong executive. The prime minister enjoyed no independent powers and served, like the other ministers, at the pleasure of the president. The judiciary represented a theoretical check on the executive, but in practice the newly-appointed judges were to prove responsive to the president who appointed them. Moreover, the president's control of patronage gave him a lever with the Assembly.

Broad emergency clauses in the constitution also contributed to a concentration of power in the executive. Article 57 directed:

"When in time of civil war, or in a dangerous situation arising from foreign relations, or in case of a natural calamity, or on account of a grave economic or financial crisis it is necessary to take urgent measures for the maintenance of public order and security, the President shall have the right to issue orders having the effect of law or to make necessary financial dispositions; provided, however, that the President shall exercise such powers exclusively if time is lacking for the convocation of the National Assembly. Such orders of dispositions shall be reported without delay to the National Assembly for confirmation. If confirmation of the National Assembly is not obtained, such orders shall lose their effect. . . ."[5]

The new constitution delegated little authority to other than the national government. Key functions such as police and public works would be handled from Seoul, while local organizations were merely to "perform their administration within the framework of laws and orders and . . . perform such additional tasks as are delegated to them by law." Also, while civil rights were nominally guaranteed, there were loopholes such as Article 13, which provided that "citizenship shall not be subjected to any restrictions on the freedom of speech, press, assembly, and association except as specified by law." It was a document which lent itself to manipulation.

On August 15, 1948, the third anniversary of V-J Day, the American flag was lowered in front of the capitol building in Seoul and the Korean flag raised in its place. General Douglas MacArthur flew over from Tokyo to witness the transfer of governing authority to the new Republic of Korea government.

The United Nations Temporary Commission prepared its report. The commission placed its weight firmly behind the new government, though with little realization of the momentous consequences of its action. On December 12, the United Nations General Assembly declared that "there has been established a lawful government (the government of the Republic of Korea) having effective control and jurisdiction over that part of Korea where the Temporary Commission was able to observe and consult and in which the great majority of the people of Korea reside; and that this government is based on elections which were a valid expression of the free will of the electorate of that part of Korea and which were observed by the Temporary Commission; and that this is the only such government in Korea."[6]

Korea was at least half free.

8: Darkening Skies

ON JULY 17, 1948, Syngman Rhee signed his country's new constitution in his capacity as chairman of the Assembly. The election of a chief executive by the Assembly was a formality; on July 19, Rhee was elected president of the new republic by 180 votes to 16, for Kim Koo. The vice presidency went to Lee Si-yung, an octogenarian representative of a respected noble family but a person of little political influence.

Rhee met his first opposition from the legislature in filling the post of premier. His first choice was Lee Yun-young, who enjoyed a considerable following among North Korean refugee groups but who suffered from a reputation as an extreme rightist. Lee was not acceptable to several groups within the Assembly, and in a compromise move the premiership went to Lee Bum-suk, a former general in the Chinese Nationalist Army and founder of South Korea's most powerful patriotic society, the Racial Youth Corps. There were those who speculated that Lee Bum-suk had always been Rhee's choice as premier, and Lee Yun-young only his "stalking horse."

The new premier was not alone among Rhee's appointees in having a strong rightist tinge. The foreign ministry went to Chang Taik-sang, an English-educated Ph.D. of pronounced anti-Communist views. The education ministry went to Ahn Ho-sang, a onetime professor in a German university whose views had been strongly colored by time spent in Nazi Germany. As his first task,

Ahn set about organizing a Student's National Guard, to root out leftists and to "investigate the thought trends of students."[1]

Most other ministries went to rightists of rather undistinguished abilities. Louise Yim, an American-educated independence worker who had lobbied for Korea at the United Nations, was named minister of commerce. Yun Chi-hyung, a lawyer for Rhee's Korean Commission before World War II, became home minister. The one exception to the conservative complexion of the cabinet was Minister of Agriculture Cho Bong-am, a one-time Communist who, while estranged from Moscow, retained socialistic views concerning the need for land reform in South Korea. Cho shortly broke with Rhee and became a bitter political rival.

Foreign observers were generally unimpressed with Rhee's appointments. The United Nations Temporary Commission reported that "there was widespread criticism of the personnel appointed to the Cabinet and the feeling was expressed that the President had failed to utilize fully the best talents available." This was a serious indictment, since four decades of Japanese rule had inhibited the development of leadership among the Koreans, and the new nation needed badly to make maximum use of what it had. But Syngman Rhee apparently saw his first task as the consolidation of his own position in the presidency. With this end in mind, Rhee found subordinates who did too little preferable to those who might do too much.

In the early months of his administration Rhee scrutinized his appointees for any tendency to develop an independent following within the administration. Within months of taking office, Rhee initiated the first of the periodic cabinet shake-ups which were to become a hallmark of his administration. First to go were Foreign Minister Chang, Home Minister Yun, and National Police Director Cho Byong-ok. If Rhee's original appointments had been uninspired, those which followed became even more so. In the absence of capable advisors, virtually all decisions in both policy and administrative matters were made by the president himself—the beginning of a vicious circle in which Rhee became so occupied with trivia that he was unable to supervise an orderly process of decision-making.

In North Korea the Communists, too, faced a shortage of trained administrators and skilled labor. Policy direction, however, was not lacking. Acting under directions from Moscow, and aided by Soviet technicians, the Kim Il-sung regime set about increasing industrial production and building up a military machine. The Communists were stung by the holding of separate elections in South Korea, and anti-American and anti-Rhee propaganda from the north became increasingly bitter. To counter the effect of the South Korean elections, Pyongyang announced in July 1948 that it would hold elections on August 25 to fill a 572-man legislature. Following a Communist-style "election," the new Supreme People's Assembly ratified a constitution modeled after those of the European satellites. On September 10, the assembly gave unanimous approval to a cabinet appointed by Kim Il-sung, and the Democratic People's Republic of Korea came into being.

Like the Rhee government, the D.P.R.K. claimed to be the sole legal government for Korea. In fact, however, there could be no comparison between South Korea, formed under U.N. auspices through reasonably democratic processes, and the Communist regime imposed on North Korea by the Soviets. In addition to this, there were other interesting dissimilarities.

"The cabinet of the [R.O.K.] government drew heavily upon the small group of Western-educated Koreans for its personnel. The members of the northern body were generally much less cosmopolitan in their background. The college- and university-trained members of the northern body had received their education almost exclusively in Japan and Korea. . . . Both governments contained many persons who had served prison terms under the Japanese and had been active against the Japanese regime at one time or another, although the northern government probably contained a larger number of actual revolutionaries."[2]

The rise of Syngman Rhee in South Korea must have been particularly galling to the Soviets and Korean Communists, in that Chinese Communist successes on the mainland in late 1948 held forth the promise of an East Asia totally under Communist rule. Only South Korea appeared to stand in the way. Unsuccessful in their initial efforts to subvert South Korea, the Communists tried a new tactic: Pyongyang "requested" that Soviet troops be withdrawn from North Korea. The Communists' plan was transparently clear, but it was ultimately to achieve its goal. When the Soviets replied that their troops would be withdrawn by the end of 1948, it signalized the beginning of a worldwide campaign to force the withdrawal of American troops from Korea.

The first uneasy year of South Korean independence was notable for the appearance of serious economic shortcomings. South Korea contained the larger proportion of arable land in Korea and was historically Korea's rice bowl. However, even agriculture was strained by the continued influx of refugees from the North; over a million Koreans are known to have entered South Korea from North Korea, Manchuria, and China in the three years after liberation, and as many as a million more may have entered through other than official entry stations.[3] Although many of the refugees came from the better-educated classes in the north, jobs were so scarce in South Korea that many were forced to live in the streets and slums.

With most of Korea's industry located in the north, the gap between R.O.K. exports and even its most essential imports could not be closed. Rhee's unwillingness to trade with Korea's former master, Japan, was a boon to smugglers and cut off a needed source of tariff revenue. An acute shortage of consumer goods kept prices in a perpetual spiral, undermining the value of the South Korean currency. Under military government, $6,000,000 in U.S. aid was provided Korea in 1945–46, $93 million in 1946–47, and $113 million in 1947–48. But such aid was not sufficient in a country whose economy had been as severely dislocated as South Korea's, though it was self-evident that the Rhee administration could be doing more to help itself.

It was unfortunate for his country that Rhee's background was more in the field of political maneuvering and diplomacy than in economics and administration. Not until 1950, and only then under heavy pressure from the United States, did Rhee come to grips with the serious inflation threatening his country. Moreover, while the North Koreans had enacted a land reform law in 1946 which gained them considerable initial popularity, Rhee hesitated to antagonize Korea's conservative landowners, and no land-reform legislation was enacted in South Korea until the spring of 1950. Fortunes were made, however, by businessmen able to gain control of former Japanese properties. Homes, industries, and land holdings were sold by the government to pro-administration businessmen, usually after substantial bribes to officiating bureaucrats.

Thus the summer of 1948 saw Rhee consolidating his position in the Korean presidency, but with the stability of his administration threatened internally by economic weakness and corruption, and externally by the Communist threat, which often materialized in the form of riots and border raids. The task of guiding South Korea's fortunes would have taxed the abilities of younger and more skilled statesmen than Rhee; as it was, growing rivalry between a quick-tempered executive and a prerogative-conscious legislature made for little political teamwork in Seoul. From his hillside mansion, Kyungmudae, Rhee fought to prevent his ministers from being interrogated by the Assembly concerning ministerial affairs. In the faction-ridden Assembly, various groups worked on behalf of landowners and mining interests but almost no one for the welfare of Korea as a whole. Throughout the government, officials reverted to centuries-old practices in supplementing their meager salaries with bribes. In Korea everyone was protecting his own interests, and if there was any altruistic footnote it was Rhee himself. Even as he moved to monopolize political power, he did so in the genuine belief that whatever strengthened his hand was ultimately good for Korea.

In the international field, a question with which Rhee was forced to come to grips was that of an American troop withdrawal from

South Korea. During his visit to the United States, in his anger at General Hodge, Rhee had demanded that America withdraw its forces from South Korea. In July 1948, however, he wrote to friends:

" . . . I was told the U.S. Army is making plans to withdraw during the next 60 or 90 days. Our position in that connection is that they ought to give us time in which to organize our national defenses. When that is done they can do what they please. . . . Americans should first decide to safeguard the United States interests in Korea, first from a sense of moral obligation, and second for the sake of American security. If the American people are sufficiently informed of these facts, I do know the Americans will not pull out."[4]

Rhee recognized the threat to the north, and swallowed his pride to the extent of requesting that U.S. troops remain in Korea. But he continued to damage his cause with periodic threats to unify Korea by force, threats which prompted the Pentagon to provide Rhee's constabulary with only such light weapons as it deemed necessary for defensive purposes. There was fault, actually, in both Seoul and Washington. The *New York Times* editorialized:

"Dr. Syngman Rhee, President of Korea, wants to know: 'In case of an attack by an outside power, would the Republic of Korea be able to count on all-out American military aid? That is a fair question and deserves an answer free from double-talk. The United States has already announced that it proposes to withdraw its armed forces from Korea in the near future. But, says Dr. Rhee, ' We do not believe that the United States can or will withdraw its remaining troops until it has answered the question as to what will be done in case the Communists attack across the 38th Parallel.' "

In Washington, of course, there was reason to be vague. Some observers feared that, if assured of U.S. support in the event of hostilities, Rhee might provoke an incident along the border in order to bring about American intervention. But it was also true that the American military withdrawal—stemming from the announced Soviet pullout—left South Korea facing superior Communist forces on the peninsula which could be supplied and reinforced overland from the U.S.S.R. The *Times* went on:

"There has been quite a bit of discussion about some form of Pacific security pact, most of it in very general terms, that would afford something of a counterpart to what has been done in Europe. . . . But the biggest single obstacle to even the start of Pacific security discussions is the lack of any clear statement of interest and purpose on the part of the United States. . . . The United States, while proclaiming that it will assist European nations, such as Greece, for example, to defend themselves against aggression, has indicated quite clearly that there is no intention in the Administration of following a corresponding course in China. . . . More than one bewildered Asiatic, and for that matter American, has asked just what was the intent of a policy that offered aid to Greece if it kept the Communists out and denied it to China unless it were willing to let the Communists in."[5]

By the fall of 1949, North Korea was well along in the training of the 500,000-man army which would strike south the following summer. Against a background of threats from Radio Pyongyang, Communist patrols made reconnaissance raids across the thirty-eighth parallel in considerable force. On occasion, towns several miles south of the parallel were seized and held briefly by Communist raiders before they withdrew to North Korea. But such raids had been going on for some time, and the unreliability of R.O.K. statistics made their scope and frequency difficult to evaluate.

By the end of 1947, the American-trained Korean constabulary had an authorized strength of 20,000 men. The aid program was stepped up the following year, and arms and equipment were provided for an army of 50,000; domestic criticism of the Truman administration for "losing" China was spurring Washington to cover its tracks with respect to Korea. Within the Pentagon, however, Korea was widely viewed as a strategic liability. As early as May 1947 Secretary of War Patterson "reiterated that we should get out of Korea at the earliest possible time. He stressed the expense to the United States and the insignificance of the strategic and economic value of Korea. General Marshall did not agree with these views."[6]

Those who felt that South Korea was not badly off in terms of military strength pointed out that the former constabulary, which now constituted the R.O.K. Army, was not the only military organization in the country. The South Korean police numbered 30,000, and were almost as well armed as the army. Various paramilitary forces such as the Racial Youth Corps were felt to provide a reserve for any national mobilization. In addition to the border raids which continued to harass its northern border, however, the R.O.K. was now confronted with a threat which would plunge it into a period of terror to be exceeded only by the Korean War period itself.

On the night of October 19, 1948, a R.O.K. Army regiment stationed in the town of Yosu, on the southwest tip of Korea, mutinied and killed its officers. Seemingly led by Communists, the insurgents won over a large segment of the civil populace by urging revenge against the local police. As at Taegu, the brutality of the police, many of whom were holdovers from the Japanese occupation, earned them the fury of leftist-led mobs. Spreading rumors that all Korea had fallen to the Communists, the insurgents marched twenty miles inland to capture the town of Sunchon. Here, however, loyal troops checked the advance and dealt summary punishment to the rebels. Sunchon was recaptured on October 22, and five days later loyal troops entered Yosu.

The near-extinction of civil liberties in South Korea which followed the Yosu rebellion stemmed from recognition that the internal Communist threat had not yet been destroyed. Rumors of imminent invasion from the north were widespread, and it seemed that only the police were demonstrably loyal to the government. R.O.K. spokemen estimated that two thousand persons had been killed in the uprising. In a burst of xenophobia, Premier Lee Bum-suk contrasted the proven loyalty of the police with the disloyalty of the army at Yosu, and declared that he had warned the Americans that failure to screen the recruits would make a "Trojan horse" of the army.[7]

An estimated eight thousand persons were arrested in the wake of the Yosu rebellion, often on the flimsiest of charges. A proclamation warned that "the police will, without hesitation, shoot anyone who scatters handbills or in any way incites people to riot. Citizens are requested not to stand too near these dangerous elements." Student committees were set up in schools to report on politically unreliable elements and those who did not firmly support the Rhee regime.[8]

Ten months after the Yosu rebellion, persons were still being executed for alleged complicity in the uprising. The terror which followed in the wake of Yosu stemmed in part from genuine panic, but otherwise was scarcely different from any comparable period in Nazi Germany or Stalinist Russia. A member of Rhee's cabinet, Louise Yim, has confessed her disapproval of the action.

"Not all those executed by the Republic were enemies. . . . One day a member of a firing squad came to me with a message from Prof. T.S. Kim, his last message before being taken out for execution.

"I cannot believe that Prof. Kim was a traitor. During the Japanese occupation, he was one of the few who defied them by teaching Korean history and writing important studies of our history while teaching at Seoul University. . . . He was a man of peace, a pacifist who could not raise his hand against his fellow man."[9]

Meanwhile, the fact that South Korea's leftists had been driven underground in no way inhibited politics as usual on the right. Although Rhee's conservative opponents were as anti-Communist as he himself, this fact did not make for political harmony; in fact the absence of significant ideological differences tended to encourage rather than inhibit bickering over minor issues, as did Rhee's penchant for disparaging any opponent as pro-Communist. But with new Assembly elections scheduled for 1950, Rhee's followers in the legislature faced an uncertain future. Although they represented the largest single bloc in the Assembly, they still occupied only a third of the seats and had become associated with a number of unpopular policies during their two years in office.

Apart from party label, the Assembly was jealous of its prerogatives and sensitive to any executive usurpation of its powers. The Assembly's effectiveness as a check on Rhee, however, was limited by its disunity and by the administration's ability to "buy" votes on crucial issues. Even as war threatened from the north and disaffection from within, Assembly leaders girded themselves for a campaign which would be fought as bitterly as any in the Korean War: the struggle between Rhee and the Assembly for political supremacy.

In April 1949, Rhee embarked on his most ambitious stumping tour of Korea. From the platform of his private train he spoke to crowds from Seoul south to Pusan, rested in the port town of Chinhae, and then worked his way north from Mokpo back to Seoul. For a septuagenarian the tour was no mean feat. Everywhere Rhee's simply-phrased orations on unification were greeted by enthusiastic crowds. Rhee returned to Seoul convinced more than ever that he spoke for the Korean people.

There remained, however, one other who thought that he, too, spoke for the Korean people. The volatile Kim Koo had lived in political eclipse since his unsuccessful opposition to South Korean elections, and since then had heard himself and Kim Kyu-sic denounced by Rhee as "traitors" who were being "used by the Communists." He nonetheless retained a considerable following among the Korean Independence Party and other rightist groups, and, unlike the gentle Kim Kyu-sic, was personally capable of attempting a coup against the Rhee regime.

On June 29, 1949, a Korean Army lieutenant, said to be a member of the K.I.P., gained admittance to Kim Koo's study, where he shot the old revolutionary four times. Kim died almost instantly, and the assassin was rescued only after having been beaten senseless by Kim's bodyguards. Rhee declared himself "deeply shocked," observing that he had hoped "the day would soon come when Mr. Kim Koo realized that I had no personal ambition, and that my opinions are an expression of what I feel points the way . . . toward the sound development of Korea."[10] Almost immediately, however, there were indications that this was not one of Korea's "spontaneous" assassinations.

The violent ends which had befallen other of Rhee's rivals such as Lyuh Wun-hyung and Song Chin-woo not surprisingly triggered rumors that the administration was behind the assassination. Rhee himself felt compelled to issue a disclaimer, stating that "facts will show that Mr. Kim Koo's death was the direct result of divergences of opinion with his own party." On July 2, however, R.O.K. military police arrested the editor of a Seoul daily for printing the statement of a Korean Independence Party spokesman that police reports concerning the assassin's motives did not agree with evidence uncovered by party investigators. The assassin, kept incommunicado by the military police, was tried in secret and sentenced to life imprisonment.*

Threatened by the Communists on all sides, and suspicious of the motives of many of his own appointees, Rhee struck out at his enemies as best he could. The Yosu area continued to be the scene of sweeping reprisals; as late as August 1949, sixty-four persons were executed for alleged complicity in the rebellion. When opposition newsmen charged to the U.N. Commission that Rhee was using the Yosu trials as a means of destroying his conservative opposition, Rhee ordered five newsmen arrested. So haphazard had Rhee become in his charges, and so reckless in his campaign against the Communists, that when Pyongyang radio threatened on October 17 to unite Korea "by its own forces" there were those in South Korea who looked to the north for liberation.

* *New York Times* July 3, 1949. Kim's assassin, Ahn To-hi, served only about three years of his life term. He was pardoned at some time during the Korean War and is reportedly now a lieutenant colonel in the R.O.K. Army.

9: June 25, 1950

IT IS A truism that, in terms of the East-West struggle, the Korean War has taken on a significance which belies its military indecisiveness. The fact that it was essentially a test of will between the Free World and the Communist bloc has overshadowed the fact that it was fought on a strategically obscure peninsula with weapons which were largely obsolescent in the nuclear age. Both sides fought under self-imposed restraints, lest this localized war erupt into World War III: the United Nations Command refrained from attacking targets in Manchuria, while the Communists made no effort to attack vital Allied staging areas in Japan.

The repercussions of the Korean War were, however, enormous. For Communist apologists in the West, the use of direct force by the bloc in its attempt to complete the communization of North Asia destroyed a cherished illusion, that whereas communism would attempt to expand its borders by means of subversion and revolution it would not resort to military aggression. And as an exposé of Communist brutality the Korean War has been equaled only by the Hungarian Revolution.

Militarily, the Korean War held lessons for both sides. The North Koreans found it impossible to drive an enemy inferior in both numbers and equipment completely off the peninsula. The Chinese Communists erred in a gamble that, if committed in sufficient numbers, their armies would succeed where the North Koreans had failed. On the other hand, the ability of the Communist forces to hold at bay the American-led U.N. Command tended to boost Peking's stock throughout Asia. And in America, the indecisive character of the Korean War triggered a controversy over the feasibility of limited-objective warfare which has scarcely abated a decade later.

Overriding all other considerations, however, was the fact of Communist aggression and the Free World decision to meet the challenge. The establishment of a United Nations Command, a diplomatic and propaganda success made possible by Moscow's boycott of the United Nations during June and July 1950, was a fitting sequel to President Truman's decision that America must meet Communist force with force. The decision to defend South Korea with American lives remains the greatest demonstration to date of America's intent to contain Communist aggression.

What, then, prompted the aggression which was to result in one of the few setbacks to Communist expansion in Asia? The full answer may not be known to this generation. Indeed, even speculation is made difficult by the fact that the Soviets appear to have taken unjustifiable risks to gain control of a small section of Far Eastern real estate.

It is possible that occupation of Korea became an objective of Soviet policy late in World War II. President Truman has related how, at Potsdam, General Antonov, the Soviet Army chief of staff "showed particular interest in any intentions we might have to undertake operations against the Kuriles or in Korea. . . . Gen. Marshall stated that we had no present plans for amphibious operations against Korea. From our point of view, he explained, such a move would require an undue amount of shipping, and it was the belief of our experts that Korea could be brought under control without difficulty once our aircraft could operate from fields on the Japanese island of Kyushu."[1]

Nonetheless, it is difficult to imagine South Korea as an objective for which the Soviets would be prepared to risk war. Whereas North Korea included the Japanese-built complex of power dams along the Yalu, the Orient's largest fertilizer factory at Hungnam, and numerous other industries, South Korea was but a rice producer with very limited industrial potential. It appears likely that at the end of World War II the Soviets were only nominally interested in South Korea. General Order No. 1, which instructed MacArthur to occupy Korea up to the thirty-eighth parallel, was accepted in substance by Stalin when it was passed to him on August 16, 1945. Had South Korea been a major Soviet objective, Stalin might have pointed out that Soviet troops had entered Korea four days earlier and planned to occupy the whole peninsula.

It appears probable that, having gained U.S. acquiescence to their occupation of Korea's industrial north, the Soviets were not disposed to quarrel over American occupation of the south. Had they wished to occupy the whole peninsula, the United States might well have hesitated to make Korea the issue over which to quarrel with so recent an ally.

Why, then, the Communist onslaught five years later? One factor to be noted is that Western moves to check the advance of communism in Europe had achieved some success by 1950, first in the case of American aid to Greece and Turkey, and then with the more extensive Marshall Plan. The Berlin airlift, also, had represented a propaganda setback to the Soviets. Asia, on the other hand, had seen impressive Communist advances culminating in the retreat of the Chiang Kai-shek government to Formosa in 1949. To Stalin, as to many a czarist despot, a setback in the West may have been the cue for expansion to the East.

A second factor was probably the formal inauguration of the Republic of Korea. It was one thing to permit the Americans to accept the surrender of Japanese troops in Korea; it was another to have to endure taunts and threats from an anti-Communist regime which proclaimed itself the legitimate government of all Korea. Any concern which Moscow may have felt concerning the new government of South Korea must certainly have been fanned by Communist zealots in Pyongyang. Had not the Soviets promised them that *they* would be the rulers of Korea after liberation?

The military situation in Korea seemingly encouraged exploitation by the Communists. Moscow's policy of ruling through a puppet regime in North Korea required military backing, and this had been provided. Syngman Rhee's threats from the south had resulted in further strengthening of the "People's Army." At the same time, the South Korean penchant for crying wolf concerning invasion from the north made it seem likely that the Americans would discount reports concerning a military buildup in the north. Rhee's bellicosity made it seem possible that responsibility for initiating hostilities could be attributed to South Korea.

The one imponderable would appear to be the attitude of the United States. The Americans had been the virtual sponsors of the Syngman Rhee government, and still had a large advisory group working with the South Korean army. But the Communists received reassurances from an unexpected source. In a speech before the National Press Club on January 12, 1950, Secretary of State Dean Acheson ticked off America's "defense perimeter" in Asia: the Aleutians, Japan, Okinawa, and the Philippines. As for other areas in the Pacific, initial reliance in case of attack "must be on the people attacked . . . and then upon the commitments of the entire civilized world under the charter of the United Nations."[2] Thus were South Korea and Formosa in effect placed outside that belt of nations against whom aggression would automatically be resisted by the United States.

It appears improbable that Communist aggression in Korea was a direct result of the Acheson speech. But his National Press Club address appeared to be a definitive statement of American policy in the Pacific, one which took the guesswork out of any attempt to anticipate the American reaction to Communist adventures in the Far East. One can scarcely blame the Communists for regarding the American decision to intervene in Korea as nothing short of treachery; the world can only be grateful that World War III did not result from the Communists' miscalculation of American intentions. Soviet astonishment at the Western intervention in

Korea was probably underscored by fears of an American nuclear attack on the Soviet Union itself.

Although the Acheson speech was prompted largely by broad strategic considerations, it was delivered at a time when the United States was reappraising the extent to which it should underwrite the growing pains of the Republic of Korea. In May 1949, the Truman administration had submitted a proposal for $150 million in aid for Korea. Syngman Rhee was outspoken in criticism of the small amount of aid being provided his country, and Congress was also unhappy, though for a different reason. It delayed, amid much grumbling about "pouring money down a rathole," until on January 19, 1950—exactly a week after Acheson's National Press Club speech—it defeated the measure by a single vote. The final vote reflected both criticism of the administration's failure to grant similar aid to the Chinese Nationalist regime on Formosa, and a feeling that it was not worthwhile to provide large-scale military aid to an area which the United States was not prepared to defend militarily. Several weeks later, however, after considerable prodding by the administration, Congress passed a bill providing aid for both South Korea and Formosa which authorized $120 million in short-term aid to South Korea.

While the Rhee government continued to stress the danger of a Communist invasion, U.S. authorities took issue with Rhee over two matters, the administration's failure to act vigorously against inflation and its stated intention to postpone the Assembly elections scheduled for May, 1950. In an *aide memoire* in April, Secretary Acheson threatened to review the Korean aid program unless anti-inflationary measures were forthcoming, and expressed concern regarding Rhee's intention of postponing elections. With the R.O.K. threatened for the first time in its pocketbook, Rhee's response was gratifying: taxes would be raised as an anti-inflationary measure, and elections would be held on schedule.[3]

Rhee was, in fact, not at all anxious to hold elections. He had split with the Korean Democratic Party the previous year over issues of patronage, after that group had charged him with ingratitude for the support it had given him for the presidency. In late 1949, Assembly Speaker P. H. Shinicky and one-time National Police Director Cho Byong-ok had merged the K.D.P. with other conservative elements to form the anti-Rhee Democratic Nationalist Party. In the Assembly the new party called for a constitutional amendment to make the cabinet responsible to the Assembly, and in general moved to curb the power of the presidency. Independents on the political scene, appalled by the excesses of Rhee's campaign against the domestic left, tended to favor some check on the executive. A major fight was in prospect.

The first skirmish went to Rhee's opponents. When elections were held on May 30, the result was a resounding defeat for the administration. Rhee's following in the Assembly dropped from fifty-six to twelve, and even including pro-administration independents he could count on only about sixty-five votes. Almost immediately the Democratic Nationalists set about reintroducing a measure to make the cabinet responsible to the National Assembly. But, like Rhee, they reckoned without a stealthy military buildup in North Korea whereby the Communists had massed 100,000 men with heavy weapons behind the hills that lined the thirty-eighth parallel.

Before dawn on June 25, 1950, a light rain was falling along the border which separated South Korea from the Communist north. In Washington, "where a new stack of intelligence reports on North Korean invasion threats had been received, discounted and filed away,"[4] it was still Saturday, the 24th. President Harry Truman was out of town, vacationing in Independence. In the half-empty Pentagon, duty officers longed for an afternoon on the golf course.

At about 4:00 a.m. in Korea, an ominous rumble, not quite like a thunderstorm, sent South Korean sentries peering through the mist. Some decided it was thunder, but to those in front of six invasion corridors across the waist of Korea the noise was all too evidently the sound of Communist artillery. By 5:00, Communist infantrymen and tanks had struck across the parallel. R.O.K. sentries ran to field telephones, or just ran. Within hours the attack had overrun the first South Korean outposts and captured the city of Kaesong across the border. Radio Pyongyang shrilled that its forces had "repelled" an attack by the South Korean "puppet" army.

"Roaring, rough-skinned tanks and artillery and mortar barrages threw terror into some South Korean troops. Others fought valiantly with grenades, rifles, anti-tank guns, and dynamite charges to stop the armored drive, but the tanks came on. . . .

"The confusion was greater than the most pessimistic American advisor had feared. Units failed to report their positions to higher commands, and when they did report they often claimed face-saving victories. Officers led many a panicky retreat. Equipment which could not be replaced for months was abandoned to the Reds."[5]

For all of Rhee's statements warning of a Communist attack, consternation was as great at Kyungmudae as anywhere on June 25. But no one anticipated the speed with which the invasion would roll down the peninsula. While American officialdom in Washington and Tokyo pondered whether this was the real thing or merely another border raid, Rhee ordered all-out resistance. Ambassador Muccio assured the U.N. Temporary Commission that the R.O.K. Army would give a good account of itself.

Meeting with the U.N. Commission, Rhee first rejected the Communist charge that his country had initiated hostilities. Conscious of the importance of identifying North Korea as the aggressor, and by no means certain that the United States would come to his aid, Rhee agreed to a suggestion that the U.N. Commission appeal for a cease fire. Then—doubtless with bitter memories of the Korean emperor's fruitless appeals to Theodore Roosevelt—Rhee cabled a plea to President Truman:

" . . . We again thank you for your indispensable aid in liberating us and in establishing our Republic. As we face this national crisis, putting up [a] brave fight, we appeal for your increasing support and ask that you at the same time extend effective and timely aid in order to prevent this act of destruction of world peace."[6]

At the front, R.O.K. defenses collapsed with bewildering rapidity. From MacArthur's headquarters in Tokyo came disturbing news.

" . . . Piecemeal entry into action vicinity Seoul by South Korean Third and Fifth Divisions has not succeeded in stopping the penetration recognized as the enemy main effort . . . with intent to seize the capital city of Seoul. Tanks entering suburbs of Seoul. . . .

"South Korean units unable to resist determined Northern offensive. Contributory factor exclusive enemy possession of tanks and fighter planes. South Korean casualties as an index to fighting have not shown adequate resistance capabilities or the will to fight and our estimate is that a complete collapse is imminent."[7]

On June 27, President Truman upset Soviet calculations with his historic decision to extend U.S. air and naval support to South Korea, and to extend protection to Formosa. "The attack upon Korea," stated Truman, "makes it plain beyond all doubt that communism has passed beyond the use of subversion to conquer independent nations and will now use armed invasion and war." In South Korea, continued bad news from the front could not dampen exultation at the news that help was forthcoming, although it was also on June 27 that the South Korean government was forced to evacuate Seoul and set up a temporary capital at Taejon. To Syngman Rhee, President Truman's announcement held forth the promise of American involvement on a scale which would drive the Communists from his land, and extend the Republic of Korea from Cheju to the Yalu.

From Taejon, Rhee exhorted his countrymen to drive out the invader, but to no avail. Seoul fell on June 28, and R.O.K. forces retreating south of the Han River suffered heavy losses when Korean Army engineers prematurely dynamited the main highway bridge while most R.O.K. forces were still on the other side.

9. Memorial statue of Syngman Rhee, dedicated in Seoul, August 28, 1956. The monument, eighty-one feet in height—one foot for each year of Rhee's life at the time it was erected—provided a revealing commentary on the leader's exaggerated sense of his own greatness. (*Pacific Stars and Stripes Photo*)

Rhee now recalled his warnings of Communist strength, insisting that his country had "nothing to stop those tanks," and that American aid was "too little, too late." On June 30, Truman announced that MacArthur had been authorized to use American ground troops in Korea.

In Tokyo, MacArthur decided to examine the Korean situation at first hand. Even as the first American F-84 jets searched for North Korean supply columns, MacArthur's famed transport, the *Bataan,* touched down at Suwon, south of Seoul. After conferring there with Rhee and Ambassador Muccio, MacArthur took a jeep to the front. What he saw was not encouraging: R.O.K. soldiers were streaming south, leaderless and disorganized. Even then MacArthur underestimated the task ahead: he remarked to newsmen that two American divisions in support of the R.O.K. Army should be sufficient to "hold South Korea."[8]

Seven days after the initial North Korean invasion, the first elements of the American 24th Division landed at Pusan. Eighth Army commander Lieutenant General Walton H. Walker was placed in command of U.S. troops in Korea, and later given command of all R.O.K. troops. As the main North Korean column continued its advance down the Seoul-Taejon corridor, the first U.S. units were sent forward to fight a delaying action. Although the Americans were scarcely better equipped than the R.O.K. soldiers to cope with North Korean armor, they succeeded in delaying the advance and in forcing the Communists into time-consuming deployments. But Taejon fell on July 20; the commander of the 24th Division, Major General William Dean, was captured; and the Americans sought desperately to reorganize shattered R.O.K. units about those divisions in the south which had escaped the brunt of the North Korean offensive.

Those members of the South Korean government who had reached Taejon from Seoul now moved on to Pusan. But Rhee felt the government should stay close to the front, and after a week in Pusan moved up to Taegu with members of his entourage. The invasion brought a respite in Rhee's political wars; politics was put aside if only for as long as it took to ascertain that the R.O.K. could retain a toehold on the Korean peninsula.

By the end of July, the Communist offensive had squeezed five R.O.K. divisions and elements of three U.S. divisions into a rectangular beachhead sixty by thirty miles, the heart of which was the east coast supply port of Pusan. But the beachhead was defensible, and the Communists' long supply lines were vulnerable to air attack. Moreover, while Syngman Rhee exhorted his countrymen to new sacrifices, plans were being laid in Tokyo for a stroke which would turn the tide against the enemy.

10: War and Peace

FOR TWO months Walker bought time on the Pusan beachhead. Making maximum use of his necessarily short lines of communication he switched units from one sector to another, propped up hard-pressed R.O.K. units, and kept open the vital supply artery of Pusan. As men and supplies flowed into the beachhead the scales gradually tipped in favor of its defenders. The Communists, dependent on supply lines that stretched clear to North Korea, were unable to sustain an offensive sufficiently powerful to break through the Allied defenses. Diplomatically, the Communists suffered a crushing setback when the U.N. denounced the North Korean attack as aggression, and fifteen nations prepared to aid the United States in its support of South Korea.

In Tokyo, meanwhile, General MacArthur had determined on a bold stroke: an amphibious landing at Inchon, west of Seoul, followed by a two-pronged attack against the Communist armies in southern Korea. Although Inchon itself had little to recommend it as the site for an amphibious operation—its thirty-foot tides permitted use of the beaches for only three hours out of every twelve—there were compensating attractions. Inchon was lightly defended, and lay only twenty-five miles from Seoul. The capital was a major psychological prize, but even more importantly it lay astride the North Korean supply lines to the Pusan perimeter.

The success of the Inchon landing on September 15-16 ushered in a new phase of the war. The capture of Kimpo airfield on the 17th allowed supplies to be brought in by air; R.O.K. Marines and elements of the U.S. 7th Division reached the outskirts of Seoul on September 19. But the Communists had ordered that Seoul be defended to the death, and not until the 28th was the capital—a blackened shell—liberated from the enemy. On the following day MacArthur and Rhee made a triumphal entry, driving by motorcade to the gutted capitol building. In a brief ceremony before American and Korean soldiers and officials, MacArthur symbolically returned the capital to Rhee and assured him that the complete liberation of his homeland was near.[1]

The expected breakthrough from the Pusan perimeter did not immediately follow the fall of Seoul. As though oblivious to the events to their rear, for a week the Communists maintained their lines to the south in the face of increasing pressure from the U.N. forces. But in the closing days of September the Communist lines collapsed, first in the west and then to the north. As South Korean troops led the pursuit of a disorganized enemy it seemed that the end might well be in sight.

The only question was where to stop, and this was one question which did not bother Syngman Rhee. Even prior to June 25, Rhee had threatened to drive the Communists out of North Korea; now, as R.O.K. divisions pushed northward up the east coast there was no question of a halt at the thirty-eighth parallel—only competition as to who would first reach the Yalu. At Lake Success, however, some delegates expressed concern over this means of taking punitive action against North Korea. The U.N. Command was on its way to clearing the enemy from South Korea; was this not enough? In the flush of victory, the temptation simply to move north and finish the job was great. But with what appeared to be an excess of caution, the United States sought a specific U.N. directive which would permit punitive action against North Korea and achieve the unification of Korea in accordance with U.N. resolutions. On October 7, the General Assembly approved a resolution calling for the destruction of the North Korean armed forces and the liberation of North Korea.[2]

To the aged Rhee, a lifelong objective appeared in sight. Mac-

Arthur called upon the North Koreans to lay down their arms, warning that unless they responded immediately he would "at once proceed to take such measures as may be necessary to enforce the decrees of the United Nations." With shouts of "On to the Yalu," South Korean troops poured across the thirty-eighth parallel.

Rhee moved quickly to capitalize on the U.N. advance across the parallel. As president it fell to him to appoint provisional governors in the Republic of Korea; he now began appointing governors to rule in his name over liberated areas of the north. But the United Nations ruled that the Rhee government had no authority north of the parallel, and the General Assembly decreed that the government of a united Korea should be determined by U.N.-supervised elections throughout Korea. Rhee bitterly opposed this ruling, on the grounds that the legitimacy of the R.O.K. had already been certified by a U.N. Commission. Liberated areas of North Korea were nonetheless kept under military administration in accordance with the U.N. directive.

On October 26, elements of the R.O.K. 6th Division reached the Yalu. It was a day of triumph, yet with a disquieting note: in their report back to Eighth Army headquarters, the South Koreans maintained that the last few miles of their advance had been in the face of heavy resistance by Chinese troops. Unfortunately, the Americans had all too often been misled by exaggerated R.O.K. claims of enemy strength, and initial reports of the Chinese intervention were generally discounted.

Nonetheless, the Chinese Communists themselves had raised some storm warnings. On September 30, the day before R.O.K. forces crossed the thirty-eighth parallel, Chou En-lai had warned that Peking would not "'supinely tolerate" an Allied invasion of North Korea. On October 8, Peking proclaimed that "the American war of invasion in Korea has been a serious menace to the security of China from its very start," and warned that China "cannot stand idly by."[3]

Although somewhat more strongly worded than usual, such

threats were not new. In MacArthur's headquarters they were widely regarded as a propaganda tactic designed to slow the U.N. advance. The U.N. Command was scarcely in a position to threaten Communist China, and its strategists doubted that the Chinese believed their own propaganda. In any case, with Allied victory apparently in sight the Chinese threat seemed a very distant one. Although South Korean commanders were cautioned against overextending themselves, MacArthur divided his own forces, sending the 10th Corps up the east coast on a large-scale cleanup operation.

The presence of Chinese troops in Korea was confirmed over October 27-28 in the form of heavy attacks against four R.O.K. divisions of the 10th Corps. The U.S. 1st Cavalry Division, sent to reinforce the South Koreans, was hit by a strong Chinese thrust. But at Eighth Army headquarters there was a painful reluctance to admit the fact of Red China's massive intervention. Not until November 6 did MacArthur announce what had occurred.

"The Communists committed one of the most offensive acts of international lawlessness of historic record by moving without any notice of belligerency elements of alien Communist forces across the Yalu River into North Korea and massing a great concentration of possible reinforcing divisions with adequate supply behind the privileged sanctuary of the adjacent Manchurian border.

"A possible trap was thereby surreptitiously laid, calculated to encompass the destruction of the United Nations Forces engaged in restoring order and the processes of civil government in the North Korean border area."[4]

Even in the face of this new threat, MacArthur hoped that the war might be brought to a close. Far from pulling back the 10th Corps from its extended position to the northeast, he ordered a general attack on both the eastern and western fronts. The lull which characterized mid-November was succeeded by a general U.N. advance on November 21–25. On the 21st, the U.S. 7th Division reached the Yalu at Hyesan; with steady advances being recorded on both the eastern and western sectors, MacArthur remarked to one of his field commanders that he hoped the enemy would enable him to keep his promise—presumably made to President Truman at Wake Island—to get his American soldiers "home by Christmas."[5] November 26 brought the launching of a new United Nations offensive.

At first the Allies made gains up to several miles. Then, on the 27th, came the deluge. The Chinese Communists counterattacked in massive force across the front, singling out R.O.K. Army divisions for attack. Soon the waves of Chinese broke through the Allied lines, and the United Nations offensive turned into a near rout. Chinese divisions struck through the gap between the main body of the Eighth Army and the 10th Corps, and for the latter the retreat became a battle for survival.

To Rhee, this sudden reversal in the course of the war came at a time when the unification of his country seemed only a matter of time. But he accepted the sudden turn of events, demanding only that the United Nations share his willingness to see the war fought to a finish. China's entry into the war served only to reaffirm in his mind that Korea could never survive among her powerful neighbors except with the firm support of some outside great power.

It was a black Christmas for the U.N. forces. As the Allied army retreated south once again, it was touch and go whether the 10th Corps could be evacuated from the east-coast port of Hungnam. Chinese troops poured across the thirty-eighth parallel, where only a few months earlier R.O.K. divisions had struck north to the Yalu. Once again the U.N. forces prepared to evacuate Seoul; on January 4, the battle-scarred capital once again passed over to the enemy. As General MacArthur said, it was a new war.

Largely obscured by the Communist military successes, however, was one of the great propaganda defeats for the Communists in the cold war. In June 1950, a sizable proportion of the South Korean population had elected to take their chances with a Communist occupation. The following January, however, in the face of the Communist advance an estimated two million Koreans streamed south with the U.N. forces. Seoul became a ghost city; its residents swamped railroad facilities, clogged roads, and hampered military movements. At Suwon, south of Seoul, nearly 100,000 Koreans jammed the railroad yards, bringing train movements to a near standstill. A people who had endured the Japanese occupation with relative patience was prepared to go to any length to avoid falling once again under Communist domination. And whatever might be said of the Rhee regime, it was regarded as preferable by far to Communist rule.

The U.N. defeat in North Korea, at a time when victory appeared in sight, was a stunning blow to the Allied powers. Despair in Korea reached all the way to Lake Success; while Communist broadcasts threatened the Allied forces with annihilation, Western diplomats sought an honorable truce. To Rhee, such thinking was an even greater danger than Communist armies. When on December 14 the United Nations called for a cease fire in Korea, Rhee blasted the move as appeasement. His concern, however, was premature; Kim Il-sung, in a bellicose address, stated that the "People's Army," aided by "Chinese volunteers," would crush the enemy throughout Korea, and drive the U.N. forces into the sea.

When the Eighth Army finally checked the Communist advance south of Seoul, it was under a new commander, General Matthew B. Ridgway. General Walker, who had led his forces out of the Pusan perimeter, had been killed on an icy mountain road when a R.O.K. Army truck pulled out of line into the path of his jeep. Ridgway counted as a major task the rebuilding of morale in his army, which had known nothing but retreat since its short-lived advance to the Yalu, and in this he found strong support in Syngman Rhee. In his memoirs Ridgway has described the retreat.

"Only a few miles north of Seoul, I ran head-on into that fleeing army . . . they were coming down the road in trucks, the men standing, packed so close together [that they] had abandoned their heavy artillery, their machine guns—all their crew-served weapons. Only a few had kept their rifles. Their only thought was to get away, to put miles between them and the fearful enemy that was at their heels. . . .

"Still, I was sure that they could be made to stand and fight again. I called on Syngman Rhee for help. I asked him if he would go up to the front with me, find these troops, talk to them and try to put some heart back in them. He agreed immediately. We flew in bitter cold, in little unheated planes, the battered old canvas-covered Cubs of World War II. The temperature aloft was close to zero, and I nearly froze, though I was bundled in my heavy GI winter gear. President Rhee flew in his native dress, in a long white cotton kimono and low shoes, without even a scarf at his neck. His wrinkled, brown old face seemed to shrivel with the cold, but he never offered a word of complaint."[6]

With the U.N. lines stabilized south of Seoul, Ridgway launched a series of probing attacks which revealed that the Communists were once again experiencing logistical difficulties as a result of their extended offensive. A new U.N. offensive gained ground in January and February until the Communists were once again forced to evacuate Seoul. The U.N. counterattack initiated the final and longest phase of the Korean War. Henceforth the fighting would be confined to the waist of Korea, with neither side able to gain a decisive advantage, or to expand the scope of the war in such a way as to bring total victory. The opposing forces had reached an equilibrium in which the tide could be turned in the favor of either side only by enlarging the war to an extent which neither side felt safe in doing. Gradually it became apparent that a resolution of the Korean fighting was more likely to be found at the conference table than on the battlefield.

Like Rhee, however, MacArthur viewed the war in terms of total victory. From Tokyo, he cabled to Washington gloomy forecasts of stalemate in Korea unless he was permitted to bomb Chinese installations in Manchuria. To dramatize his views, he advised that unless the restrictions on his activity were removed the U.N. Command "should be withdrawn from the peninsula just as soon as it is tactically feasible to do so."[7]

In Washington, however, there was still hope that a negotiated peace could be won in Korea. As Ridgway's offensive gained ground, diplomatic pressure was turned against Communist China, whose aspirations to U.N. membership had suffered a serious setback when Peking was declared an aggressor in Korea. In the wake of new evidence that the Allies could not be driven out of Korea, it was hoped that the Communists would prove more amenable to a negotiated settlement.

Yet even as the military outlook brightened, a long-smouldering dispute over the conduct of the war came into the open. General MacArthur's hostility to the general Allied desire to limit the war to the Korean peninsula was well known in Washington. In addition, his penchant for critical press pronouncements had brought forth a Joint Chiefs of Staff directive admonishing him to exercise "extreme caution in public statements." It was in spite of this warning that on March 24 MacArthur issued a statement which hinted at expanded U.N. operations in Korea, but included an offer to meet the Communist commander in the field to negotiate a truce consistent with U.N. objectives.

MacArthur's action shocked President Truman, who for the last time cautioned the general concerning his public utterances. But the message was too late; MacArthur had already despatched a letter to House Minority Leader Joseph Martin attacking the administration's policy with respect to the Korean War. Martin made the letter public on April 6. Five days later Truman relieved MacArthur of all his commands, and named Ridgway to be U.N. Commander and General James Van Fleet to command the Eighth Army.

MacArthur's ouster came as a shock to Rhee. He had always supported the general in his views on expanding the war, and his removal seemed a portent that the United Nations did not intend to fight the war to a finish. However Rhee might energize his army with the hope of unification, Korea's fate was once again being decided, not by Koreans, but by "statesmen" in foreign capitals.

He grew contemptuous of the United Nations which he judged in terms of its willingness to wage war against communism.

The Allied gains north of Seoul did not go long unchecked, and in April 1951 the Communists drove the U.N. forces back to within a few miles of the battered capital. But the West's unwillingness to fight the war to a final conclusion was matched by the Communists' inability to score significant gains against the battle-hardened Eighth Army. The struggle continued through the spring of 1951, with only minor changes in the battle map but with the U.N. forces inflicting heavy losses on the Chinese.

On June 23, in the course of a radio broadcast, the Soviet delegate to the United Nations, Jacob Malik, expressed the belief that the Korean War could be settled if the two sides were prepared to discuss an armistice. On June 25, the Chinese Communist organ, the *People's Daily,* gave qualified approval to the Malik proposals. Five days later, General Ridgway addressed his Communist counterpart to propose a time and place for initial negotiations. The Communist reply indicated a willingness to negotiate, and after further exchanges liaison officers met at Kaesong to make plans for formal talks.

Hopes for an early settlement, however, were quickly dashed. For nearly two years delegates would haggle over the location of a cease-fire line, the disposition of prisoners, an inspection system to prevent new military buildups, and arrangements for a political conference to discuss Korean unification. And meanwhile, the war would go on.

So, too, would Syngman Rhee's political wars. With Rhee's term as president due to expire in less than a year, his opponents continued to dominate the Assembly, which under the Constitution would elect the next president. Determined to overthrow Rhee in the 1952 election, his opponents in the Assembly found numerous instances of corruption and malfeasance with which to attack the administration.

Not untypical of these was the National Defense Corps scandal.

The N.D.C. had been an amalgamation of various strong-arm "youth groups" which had been organized as a military unit just before the war lest they fall under the control of Rhee's political opponents. But when the corps actually had to be thrown into the fighting, certain facts about its condition came to light. Those survivors who straggled south in the second evacuation of Seoul were in rags, and in many cases were suffering from extreme malnutrition. They brought back stories of nonexistent supplies and of being sent against the Communists without even a rifle. An investigation revealed that the N.D.C. commander, a son-in-law of the defense minister, had embezzled funds allocated for its food, clothing, and equipment.

Notwithstanding the N.D.C. debacle, Rhee continued to urge the arming of his various "youth groups" in addition to his periodic demands for the creation of new R.O.K. Army divisions. Apart from General Van Fleet, however, Rhee found the American military reluctant to entrust a greater proportion of the front to the South Koreans. In April 1951, Van Fleet himself conceded that "the basic problems with the R.O.K. Army are leadership and training. . . . It is estimated that since the beginning of the Korean campaign equipment losses in R.O.K. Army units have exceeded that necessary to equip ten divisions; this without inflicting commensurate losses on the enemy and in some cases without the semblance of a battle."[8]

As much publicized as the National Defense Corps scandal was the Kochang massacre, named for a village in southernmost Korea near Pusan. The Communist retreat from southern Korea had left isolated pockets of North Korean guerrillas and stragglers in the mountains, marauding bands which remained a threat in the countryside even after the 1953 armistice. In the course of an antiguerrilla campaign in February 1951, a R.O.K. Army detachment lost contact with a group of guerrillas near Kochang. Furious, the South Korean commander accused the villagers of harboring the fugitives. After herding the village inhabitants into a schoolyard, he ordered all the men shot, a total of about two hundred.

Word of the massacre reached Pusan, where the Assembly voted to make an investigation. Within the administration, however, there was a concerted effort to suppress the facts of the case. When an Assembly committee attempted to reach Kochang to interview survivors, they were completely frustrated by one Colonel "Tiger" Kim, a favorite of Rhee's whom the president later appointed director of the National Police. Placed in command of a picked group of R.O.K. soldiers, Kim staged a skirmish among his own men as a means of declaring the route to Kochang a battle area which could not be entered by the assemblymen. After being treated to this engagement between R.O.K. soldiers and "guerrillas," the fuming legislators were turned about and bundled back to Pusan.

It was unfortunate but characteristic of Rhee that the chief executive was too engrossed in the war and his own plans for reelection to see justice done in the Kochang affair. He was so incensed at his Assembly opponents, whom he openly denounced as pro-Communist, that almost anything seemed preferable to supplying them with damaging admissions with which to attack his administration. He had come increasingly to equate opposition to himself with pro-communism, and he felt completely justified in keeping about him the likes of "Tiger" Kim with whom to harass his enemies.

Memories are long in Korea, and Rhee was able to suppress the hatreds aroused by the Kochang massacre only so long as he stayed in power. On May 12, 1960—nine years after the incident and only weeks after Rhee was turned out of office—a local Kochang official named Park Yung-ho was seized and burned to death by a mob described as relatives of the Kochang victims. The luckless Park was charged with "failing to bring to justice" those responsible for the massacre.

Western diplomats in Seoul became increasingly critical of Rhee's domestic excesses. But the United States, on which the Rhee government was dependent for its very existence, had its hands full enough with the prosecution of the war without attempting to bring Rhee to heel. Rhee, on his part, interpreted such noninterference as a further proof that his leadership was indispensable to the Free World effort in Korea. Rhee's fan mail often supported this contention; within the United States, South Korea had succeeded to a good deal of the right-wing support which had previously been a monopoly of the Chinese Nationalists. It was understandable that, with the eyes of the world on Korea, the State Department was not disposed to draw attention to the police-state characteristics of the Rhee government. Nonetheless, America's failure to insist from the first on a standard of behavior from the Rhee administration which would justify the Allied effort in Korea would lead to further excesses as time went on.

11: Survival of the Fittest

THE WAR itself had become a stalemate. The U.N. comeback following the initial Chinese offensive had removed forever the threat of a second Pusan beachhead. On the other hand, the Eighth Army was unable to break through the Communist lines north of Seoul. Once more the Korean War posed a problem for peacemakers: was it a war to liberate Korea, or could the Allies legitimately settle for less than total victory? Himself a member of the MacArthur school, Van Fleet chaffed under directives which put severe restrictions on even local Allied offensives. Yet both the United States and the United Nations were committed to seek a settlement in the negotiations at Panmunjom, and Washington was extremely reluctant either to risk unnecessary casualties or to take military action which might not be supported by its Allies.

In the armistice negotiations themselves, progress was excruciatingly slow. Scarcely had agreement been reached on a military demarcation line when the Communists created an impasse on the issue of prisoners of war. Figures released in December 1951 had revealed that the Communists were prepared to return only a fraction of the total number of prisoners they were known to have captured. The United Nations Command demanded that the Communists account for prisoners beyond the 11,559 they were willing to return, most of whom had presumably died in captivity. But if nothing could be done for these Allied prisoners, the record of Communist barbarity served to stiffen the Allied determination that no Communist prisoner who refused repatriation would be forced to return to communism.

In South Korea, however, both the stalemated war and the truce negotiations were secondary in the eyes of many Koreans to certain matters of domestic politics—all of which concerned the re-election prospects of Syngman Rhee.

The constitution under which Rhee took office in 1948 was one which he had helped to draft, and it incorporated many features of a strong executive which he desired. But many of the features which he found useful, such as the emergency police powers which he used so freely, had been obtained through concessions to the National Assembly; one of these had been that the Assembly would have the right to elect the president. Ever since 1950, when the elections which he had held only reluctantly went against him, Rhee's support in the Assembly had dwindled. By the end of the following year, his prospects for re-election by the Assembly were regarded as nil, a fact which was a source of great comfort to his enemies.

Although Rhee periodically stated that he was not a candidate for re-election, his activities as early as the spring of 1951 belied these professions. In April 1951, he departed from his previous aloofness from partisan politics in directing the formation of an administration political party to be headed by himself. Rhee did so with obvious reluctance—his public statements continued to indicate that he regarded himself as above politics—but he appears to have recognized the need for a political vehicle behind which to mass his popular and organizational assets.

The character of the fledgling Liberal Party quickly became that of an organization dedicated solely to securing Rhee's re-election. In composition it included most of the pro-Rhee legislators in the Assembly, but it was largely dominated by the leaders of non-Assembly groups on which Rhee had come to rely for demonstrations of popular support. One such group was Rhee's old organization, the National Society—formally the National Society for the Rapid Realization of Independence. Others appealed to various

10. Syngman Rhee and Mrs. Rhee on the reviewing stand in Seoul at the celebration of Rhee's eighty-fourth birthday in 1959. Within a year of this occasion the Rhees were to hear the opening rumbles of the revolution that swept the president from power. (*Pacific Stars and Stripes Photo*)

social groups: the Korean Federation of Trade Unions, the Korean Women's Association, the League of Korean Laborers. Although not avowed political organizations, each of these was in practice an action arm of the Liberal Party.

Even while fighting raged to the north, the party organization was rushed to completion in the closing months of 1951. Rhee had marshaled his forces none too soon. When, as a trial balloon, he sent to the Assembly an amendment providing for popular election of the president instead of election by the Assembly, the measure was resoundingly defeated. Rhee knew he had a fight on his hands—how much of one even he probably did not guess. It is a peculiarity of Korean society that even at this stage Rhee could continue to disavow any interest in re-election. But Oriental nations, unfamiliar with the trappings of democracy, continue to place a premium on an attitude of humility in office seekers, and Korean observers were less critical of Rhee's apparent hypocrisy than many foreigners.

In his campaign to secure re-election, Rhee had two basic alternatives. One was to operate within the existing constitutional structure, under which the president was elected by the Assembly, but to bring such pressure to bear on the legislature that it would be forced to accept him for a second term. Factors which argued in favor of such a course were Rhee's control of the army and other means of coercing the Assembly, the vulnerability of many "opposition" legislators to administration bribes, and the fact that Rhee's objective might be secured without the bad publicity which might accompany a constitutional amendment.

Such a course, however, had one serious drawback: it in no way checked the constitutional prerogatives of the Assembly, which would presumably continue to harass his administration and to threaten the defeat of Rhee or any chosen successor four years later. In the end Rhee determined upon a frontal assault against the Assembly, one which would neutralize it as a rival to the executive. He regarded most of the assemblymen as close to traitors for having opposed him on so many occasions; his ego made the legislators' conduct appear so heinous that he was quite willing to believe that many were Communists, receiving funds from North Korea with which to oppose his re-election. If any further justification were required, Rhee doubtless told himself that the course of democracy in South Korea would be furthered by allowing the people to vote directly for their president.

Within the Assembly, Rhee's opponents girded their loins. They were, on the whole, a very mixed group in terms both of political party and motivation. Some were genuine partisans of parliamentary government who felt that a republican government patterned after that of the United States was not necessarily best for Korea. Others were simply democrats who feared that Rhee sought to entrench himself as a dictator. Some sought merely to increase their own influence and the power of the Assembly by securing the election of a less strong-willed executive. Still others opposed Rhee for tactical reasons, hoping to be bought off by the administration when their votes were needed in a showdown.

Rhee set the stage in the spring of 1952 with a series of speeches in which he equated his enemies in the Assembly with the enemy to the north: both were out to destroy him and, through him, to destroy Free Korea. The battle was not fully joined until May, however, when Rhee replaced a somewhat ineffectual home minister with the controversial Lee Bum-suk. Lee, whose Racial Youth Corps had grown in numbers and influence as a strong-arm auxiliary of the administration, was a person who could be counted upon to insure his chief's and his own political advancement. Simultaneously with Lee's appointment began "spontaneous" demonstrations calling for the re-election of Rhee to the presidency, and for the selection of Lee as his running mate.

Lee had been in office only a week when, on May 25, he initiated the crisis period by reimposing martial law in Pusan, ostensibly as an anti-guerrilla measure. The fact that the only remaining guerrillas in southern Korea were far to the west did not faze Lee or his chief, though subsequent administration pronouncements justified martial law by somewhat vaguer references to the need for a "rooting out of Communists." The Assembly, however, was not cowed by the implications of this latest threat. By a vote of ninety-six to three, but with numerous abstentions, the Assembly voted to lift martial law, in effect overriding the administration action which under the constitution had to be ratified by the Assembly.

Far from checking Rhee, however, the Assembly action only infuriated him. On May 27, forty-seven assemblymen, though presumably immune from arrest during Assembly sessions, were arrested by R.O.K. Army police, and nine of these were subsequently jailed. A presidential statement announced that "far-reaching Communist connections have been uncovered, and authorities are taking steps to make a thorough investigation." Rhee denied reports of intimidation and coercion against the legislators as "unfair stories and unfounded rumors."[1] He nonetheless ignored the Assembly's action in lifting martial law, and continued to wield the powers of his office as though the legislature did not exist.

With nine of their colleagues in jail on vague charges of conspiracy and others in hiding, the Assembly voted unanimously not to adjourn until the arrests were explained. Pro-Rhee assemblymen, a somewhat embarrassed minority, avoided the sessions. A government spokesman explained that the assemblymen did not enjoy legislative immunity from arrest, having been apprehended *in flagrante delicto*. This explanation hardly squared with the facts of the case, and charges against the nine would be dismissed following Rhee's re-election, but the incident underscored the fact that no assemblyman was immune from arrest. Mass organizations rallied to the administration cause, and on May 28, schools, shops, and markets closed down in South Korea's cities to permit a four-hour demonstration for Rhee's re-election.

Within days the crisis worsened. On May 31, Home Minister Lee announced the arrest of eleven persons, including the secretary of a leading opposition assemblyman, John M. Chang, on charges of plotting to assassinate Rhee. According to the police,

Assemblyman Chang, who was favored by many assemblymen to succeed Rhee as president, was working with the conspirators and making use of money provided by the Communists to depose Rhee and bring about unification negotiations with North Korea! The charges were preposterous, but to the uninformed Korean peasant it appeared much as though his president was fighting back valiantly against the most sinister kind of court conspiracy.

Rhee himself was using what was perhaps the best tactic open to him. By attacking his opponents with the charge of pro-communism, he was striking the one chord with which he could count on a sympathetic hearing from his Allies. As for any question of ulterior motives, Rhee continued to insist that he was not a candidate for re-election; he merely wanted to return the franchise to the people. When the vice-speaker of the Assembly submitted his resignation in protest against Rhee's "assault on the constitution," the government refused to accept his resignation. When the U.N. Commission asked that the imprisoned assemblymen be released and that martial law be lifted, Rhee simply ignored the request.[2]

By the first week of June, Pusan was an armed camp. The arrival of a fresh battalion of National Police triggered rumors that Rhee planned to dissolve the Assembly, a threat which was not without some effect. If the Assembly were indeed dissolved, every opposition assemblyman would be forced to seek re-election under rather trying circumstances—that is, if Rhee saw fit to hold new elections at all. The fact that the chief executive had already flouted the constitution on the issue of martial law in Pusan encouraged the wildest rumors of what Rhee might be planning.

Rhee's primary instrument against the Assembly continued to be the police. After the houses of opposition legislators were unexpectedly searched one night, increasing number of assemblymen chose to spend night in the Assembly hall. Conscious of the fact that his charges of pro-communism had given him the propaganda initiative, Rhee flayed the National Assembly for having "betrayed the will of the people."

Internationally, Rhee's polemics did not at first attract wide attention. On the Korean scene, they shared the spotlight not only with the fighting at the front and the negotiations at Panmunjom but with the spectacular Communist prisoner-of-war outbreaks on Koje Island. In the United States, Korean political affairs were further rivaled as news by the hotly contested presidential primaries between Taft and Eisenhower. But Rhee was not one to stay out of the news. In mid-June, after first charging that the Voice of America and the United Nations Commission had interested themselves "beyond their jurisdiction" in Korea's internal affairs, Rhee suspended all V.O.A. broadcasts from South Korean territory. In terms of his fight with the Assembly, his precipitate action against the V.O.A. was a minor sidelight. But in terms of his relations with the United States, Rhee's willingness to strike out at his protector without any attempt at temperate negotiation was an ominous sign. The V.O.A. broadcasts, possibly unwisely, had included in their news summaries Free World comment on South Korea's political crisis. But the R.O.K. reaction, which termed the broadcasts "bitterly anti-government criticism, obviously insulting,"[3] could as easily have come from Pyongyang as from Pusan.

With Rhee holding a monopoly of the police, the army, and other instruments of coercion, and having demonstrated his willingness to override the constitution when pressed, even his bitterest enemies felt compelled to examine the possibility of some form of compromise. Rhee, who wanted to break the power of the Assembly, not to dissolve it, provided some encouragement to those who favored compromise; on June 5 he sent word to the Assembly that in return for popular election of the president he was prepared to give the Assembly an increased voice in the selection of cabinet ministers. At the time he threatened openly to dissolve the Assembly if his demands were not met, observing dryly that "the will of the people is more important than the letter of the Constitution." The *Christian Science Monitor*, however, editorially described Rhee's move as "a desperate attempt to perpetuate his own political power [through] a *coup d'état* worthy of a totalitarian police state."[4]

The American government, like the *Monitor,* was more impressed by Rhee's threats to dissolve the Assembly than by the equally arbitrary acts which had preceded it. President Truman wrote to Rhee counseling against "irrevocable steps" such as dissolution. Rhee, who recognized the value of the threat of dissolution as opposed to the act, assured Truman that he would disband the Assembly only as a last resort. With the United States presumably mollified, all that remained was for the Assembly to accede to his original demands. Following a new series of popular demonstrations, Rhee announced that while he did not desire another term in office he was prepared to bow to the will of the people.

With Rhee apparently holding all the cards, a middle group in the Assembly which favored compromise increased its activity. Assemblyman Chang Taik-sang, who had been in and out of the administration but who was nominally an independent, set about giving Rhee what he wanted but with face-saving concessions to the Assembly. Progress, however, was slow; so many legislators remained in hiding that it was seldom possible to achieve a quorum. Meanwhile, the June 23 expiration date of Rhee's term of office was rapidly approaching.

Here once again the fears of many assemblymen that Rhee might actually dissolve the Assembly strengthened the executive's hand. Rather than risk a dissolution, some anti-administration legislators joined with the pro-Rhee group to argue that Rhee's term should be extended until a compromise was reached. Self-interest was so obviously paramount on both sides that one correspondent observed that "in four days' talking with Korean leaders of many factions, pro- and anti-Rhee, I have encountered no one who seemed motivated by a desire to do what is best for the Korean people."[5] Actually, many of the most stalwart anti-Rhee assemblymen were either in jail or one jump ahead of Rhee's police, and therefore scarcely able to take issue with the pro-compromise group. When, on June 20, anti-administration legislators attempted to hold a rally in a Pusan restaurant, they were attacked by pro-administration "youth" and four of them seriously injured. It therefore came as no surprise when, on June 23, the the Assembly voted sixty-one to zero to extend Rhee in office until the dispute was resolved, though Speaker P. H. Shinicky protested in vain at the obvious absence of a quorum. The *Washington Post* editorialized:

"Surely the time has come for the State Department to do more than protest the high-handed tactics of South Korean President Syngman Rhee. By means of his continuous persecution and intimidation of the National Assembly, Mr. Rhee has contrived to extend his term as President indefinitely. The best evidence of this intimidation is the fact that only 61 of 183 Assembly members —less than a quorum—were present to vote on the extension. . . .

"Two dangers are apparent in this repression. The first is that the strong-arm tactics and the persecution of other leaders will wither the resistance of the Korean people to Communist proselytizing. The second is that the impression will be conveyed that the United States and the United Nations condone Mr. Rhee's tactics. Certainly it would be too much to expect that an American-style democracy can be created in Korea. But Mr. Rhee's excesses and intransigence have made him a liability, not only to the U.N. Command, but to the free world."[6]

Rhee's extension in office was a major victory for his cause. However, the constitutional issue was hardly resolved. Although Rhee might have rushed through a similar sixty-one to zero vote re-electing him for four years, the Assembly's power would be unchecked. The next administration gambit came on June 25 when, as Rhee was delivering a speech commemorating the second anniversary of the Korean War, an elderly gentleman was seen to approach the speaker's platform and draw a pistol. Almost immediately he was buried under a phalanx of policemen. To diplomatic observers present, the "assassination attempt" appeared obviously staged, and designed to lend substance to Rhee's charges concerning a Communist plot to prevent his re-election. In accordance with R.O.K. practice, the "assailant" was kept incommunicado while police searched for evidence linking him to Rhee's opponents, and the incident provided opposition assemblymen with one more reason for staying indoors.

Making full use of the strong-arm resources of Lee Bum-suk and martial law commander Won Yong-duk, Rhee continued to browbeat the Assembly. The trial of the nine arrested assemblymen continued, in closed hearing. But Rhee's patience was growing thin; on June 29, pro-administration demonstrators held 103 assemblymen prisoner outside the Assembly hall for five hours while they harangued them and beat up one assemblyman to underscore their fidelity to Rhee. On June 30, the president warned: "I will wait only a few more days [before] I will take decisive action."[7]

On July 3, the great roundup began. The Assembly session the previous day had been attended by only 86 legislators—far short of the 123 required to amend the constitution. From Home Minister Lee went out word to the police that 65 opposition assemblymen known to be either boycotting the sessions or in hiding were to be brought to the July 5 session. To obtain the quorum of 123, the police carried out an unprecedented search for missing assemblymen. Supposed friends of legislators known to be in hiding were tempted with rewards for revealing their whereabouts, for woe to any police station unable to come up with assemblymen known to be hiding in its precinct! By midnight of July 4, 80 reluctant assemblymen had been herded to the Assembly hall, where police stood guard lest any of those who had been sleeping in the hall for protection should now attempt to escape. By dawn there were fewer than a dozen assemblymen missing, but to resolve any question of a quorum, the martial law commander released on bail all save one of the legislators supposedly on trial for treason! The ten were dutifully marched to the hall.

Rhee had won his fight. The Assembly debated into the night

on July 5, and a few strong voices were raised to call that day the final, brief hour of Korean democracy. But it became clear to all present that no one would be allowed out of the hall until Rhee's amendments were passed. By a vote of 163 to 0, with only three abstentions, the Assembly voted constitutional amendments which provided for popular election of the president and for an upper house. In return, the Assembly was given the right to vote no confidence in the cabinet, and as a sop to advocates of parliamentary government it was stipulated that the cabinet should be appointed on the recommendation of the premier. These were minor concessions, however, and in any case most of them would be withdrawn in a new series of amendments two years later.

Once his amendments were passed, Rhee's re-election was a foregone conclusion. His attention to the grass roots in 1947 and 1948 now paid dividends. Not only was there no organized group in South Korea to challenge the Liberal Party; there was no individual in wartime Korea nearly so well known as Syngman Rhee. There was, in fact, very little fight left in Rhee's opponents. Not for nearly four years would they represent anything more than a minor nuisance to Rhee and the Liberal Party.

Among the pro-Rhee factions, however, there remained considerable interest in the forthcoming "elections." Rhee was seventy-seven, and the possibility—viewed by many as a certainty—that he might die during the next four years made for considerable interest in the vice-presidential slot. Even the vice-presidential race, however, was regarded by many as a foregone conclusion. Both available and anxious for the Liberal Party nomination was Home Minister Lee Bum-suk, who had masterminded Rhee's assault on the Assembly and who in the final hour had rounded up enough assemblymen to pass the crucial amendments.

Lee was vice-chairman of the Liberal Party—Rhee of course was chairman—and by virtue of his control of the Racial Youth Corps was second in influence only to Rhee within the party. He was extremely ambitious, and he doubtless felt that his performance in the Assembly crisis had assured him of Rhee's blessing in his campaign for the vice-presidency. Unfortunately for Lee, it was the very power which he had wielded on Rhee's behalf which now caused Rhee to be very leery of permitting his home minister any further advancement. As the aging, ever-suspicious chief executive watched his minister maneuver for the vice-presidency, he recalled how Lee had retained control of the Racial Youth Corps even after, in 1948, Rhee had ordered that all private youth groups be amalgamated into a Korean Youth Corps.

There was another factor which worked to the detriment of Lee Bum-suk. By July, Rhee was getting the full backwash of the international reaction to his coup against the Assembly. Angered by what he read, Rhee tended to shift much of the blame to Lee. If there had been excesses, they were the fault of his minister. Rhee badly needed a scapegoat; if he himself had acted only from the purest motives, then it must have been Lee whose actions had brought upon South Korea such criticism from abroad.

Rhee kept his peace, but he was doubtless irritated by the action of the Liberal Party in July, which nominated Rhee for president and Lee for vice-president with almost equal enthusiasm. He determined to sabotage Lee's campaign, while running up such a vote himself as to remove any doubts about his popularity with the Korean people. After decreeing that the election campaign be limited to a period of nine days—a period so short as to place a premium on organizational strength and police backing—Rhee studiously avoided linking his own campaign with that of his Liberal Party running mate.

Rhee's ostensible rival for the presidency was Cho Bong-am, his one-time minister of agriculture, who enjoyed a measure of popularity through his advocacy of land reform measures and who was a glutton for punishment. With Rhee determined to score an overwhelming victory, the police made Cho's life so miserable that he spent most of the nine-day "campaign" in hiding. To foreign observers, the lengths to which Rhee was prepared to go to insure a landslide victory were inexplicable in terms of the threat posed by Cho. That Rhee's re-election was a foregone conclusion was reflected in the observation of a *New York Times* correspondent that "in Pusan and other cities of South Korea, voters who were queried almost invariably said that Messrs. Rhee and Lee Bum-suk were the only candidates they knew by name."[8]

As for the vice-presidential race, Rhee waited until the last minute to check the ambitions of Lee Bum-suk. Then, on the day before the election, he ordered that his followers support for the vice-presidency one Ham Tai-yong, a respected Christian layman who, at eighty-one, was the oldest and least ambitious of a handful of independent candidates for the vice-presidency. As in 1948, Rhee managed to choose a vice-president even older than himself.

In South Korea, news travels fast. Word of Rhee's eleventh-hour selection was transmitted from police station to police station in every shabby village and hamlet. The same *New York Times* correspondent in Pusan wrote on August 6: "According to reliable reports here tonight, police vehicles spent most of the day in villages and small towns carrying placards urging votes for Dr. Rhee and Ham Tai-yong."[9] Ignoring the irony of his words, Lee Bum-suk complained loudly of police interference in his campaign.

When the votes were counted on August 6, Rhee ran up over five million votes to 800,000 for Cho Bong-am. In the vice-presidential race, Rhee's hand was no less apparent. The unknown Ham Tai-yong defeated Lee Bum-suk by over 500,000 votes.

The Assembly's power was broken. Rhee's re-election was secured, and so was that of a vice-president who scarcely wished to succeed to the presidency. Rhee could now return his attention to the other war.

12: "Unification or Death"

SYNGMAN Rhee had been a revolutionary for most of his life. In a career marked by disputation, it had never bothered him to be in the minority. Although he had many times been accused of a passion to rule or ruin, no one had ever accused him of running from a fight. Having won his battle with the Assembly, Rhee in effect now took on a large segment of the Free World. Just as he had imposed his will on the National Assembly, he now set about imposing his policies on the sixteen-nation United Nations Command.

Although Rhee himself had been surprised by the intensity of his struggle with the Assembly, it is doubtful whether he ever questioned in his own mind that he would be re-elected. He was too integral a part of the Korean scene to be legislated out of his place in the sun. To Rhee, the constitutional crisis was but a distraction from the great issue of the Korean War: unification. From the time of the first negotiations with the Communists, Rhee devoted his energies to opposing any cease fire without total victory.

"Bareheaded and in a neat topcoat, the President nodded his white-haired crest at the crowd. He gestured gently with a gray felt hat in a way that must have seemed cheery to those at a distance, but it was plain at close hand that bitterness was slashed upon his crinkled brown face. . . .

" 'Time and time again,' he confessed to his people, 'I have wondered whether the Free World wants Korea to fight Communism

—or wants Korea to cease to fight.' It was a galling admission for this doughty man.

" 'The cease-fire talks,' he admitted, 'are meaningless to me.' He gripped the rail before him until knuckles paled and said, 'If necessary, Korea will fight on alone . . . to the finish! No least bit of our national territory should remain in Red hands; not a single Korean live a slave's life under Communist domination.'

"Now the great throng watched and listened in awe as their President drank of his own tears. 'I may have made a mistake,' he soberly said, 'when I ordered resistance to the Communist attack in 1950. I hoped for victory, but there is no victory though hundreds of thousands of lives have been lost.'

"There was a pause, then: 'I feel personally responsible and guilty.'

"The old man's eyes were water-veiled; his hands shook, and emotion made his vibrant voice tremble. It was not unlike an echo from the Old Testament when he went on to declaim: 'I will appear before my people and admit my mistake. I will ask our soldiers to fight on with me, though it means suicide. I will finish my days leading our men to the very end.' "[1]

In an apparent reference to his ability to inspire his soldiers, General Van Fleet had characterized Rhee as "worth his weight in diamonds." From 1952 on, however, it became apparent that Rhee was turning these same oratorical powers to defeat the U.N. objective of a peace in Korea.

At Panmunjom, the Communists at first showed little interest in a settlement, preferring to use the conference table as a vehicle for propaganda and hate-America accusations concerning germ warfare. Yet for all the discouragements, the two sides gradually inched towards agreement. The Communists finally dropped demands for a U.N. withdrawal to south of the thirty-eighth parallel, and agreed to the American sponsored line-of-contact plan for the demarcation line. Agreement was finally reached on implementation of the armistice through a Military Armistice Commission aided by joint observer teams. By the end of 1951, considerable progress had been made, although the negotiators had yet to come to grips with the momentous issue of prisoner exchange.

Shortly it appeared that the whole question of an armistice might founder on the repatriation issue. When the two sides exchanged lists of captured personnel, the naked rows of statistics were a testimonial to Communist barbarity. The U.N. list contained the names of 132,474 North Koreans and Chinese. The Communist list—for all their "victories" in the field—contained but 11,559 names, excluding about 65,000 South Koreans whom the Communists maintained had been "re-educated" and "released at the front"—that is, impressed into Communist armies. To U.N. protests concerning the discrepancy between the number of prisoners the Communists claimed to have taken and the number now offered for return, the Communists replied weakly in terms of records having been lost or "the low resistance against climate and illness" of the Americans.

Despite shock and indignation over the Communist treatment of prisoners, the negotiations continued. Concerning the repatriation issue, the U.N. Command took the position that no prisoner should be forced to return to communism against his will, as opposed to the Communist demand that all prisoners must be returned. The Communists agreed, however, to a poll of all prisoners to determine sentiment on repatriation. The results were startling.

The Americans knew that some prisoners would resist repatriation; groups of Communist prisoners periodically wrote banners in blood threatening suicide if forced to return to communism. But even the U.N. side was caught by surprise when, of over 132,000 Communist prisoners, only 70,000 desired repatriation. Two-thirds of the Chinese prisoners stated that they would not voluntarily return to their homeland, in effect preferring an uncertain future in a foreign land to life under communism. But for threats and intimidation against the prisoners by hard-core Communist cell leaders in the P.O.W. cages, the number of "non-repats" would doubtless have been even higher.[2]

When confronted with the results of the poll, Communist delegate Nam Il denounced them as "illegal" and returned to his insistence that all prisoners be repatriated. Cell leaders instigated riots in P.O.W. compounds in an attempt to lend credence to Communist charges that the Americans were coercing Communist prisoners into refusing repatriation and had "given themselves to Hitlerite tyranny and bloody terrorism." For months the denunciations continued, until in October 1952 the negotiations were abruptly recessed by General Mark Clark, who had succeeded General MacArthur following the latter's recall.

By this time the United Nations were firmly committed to the principle of no forcible repatriation. But the price paid was a high one. When the prisoner-exchange negotiations had begun in December 1951, U.N. casualties in the war had stood at 305,000. When the armistice was finally concluded in July 1953, the U.N. forces had suffered another 140,000 casualties, including nearly 9,000 American dead. The right of the individual to choose freedom was established at a terrible price.[3]

The first break in the prisoner-exchange issue came on March 1953. The talks were still in recess on February 22, 1953, when the U.N. tried a new approach by suggesting the exchange of sick and wounded by each side. At first the U.N. note went without reply; then, on March 5, Josef Stalin died in Moscow. On March 28, the Communists not only agreed to the exchange of sick and wounded prisoners, but proposed the resumption of full-dress negotiations. Once again, an armistice seemed in sight.

To Syngman Rhee, however, the implementation in April of "Operation Little Switch"—the exchange of sick and wounded—was a red flag. More and more Rhee was coming to be a barometer of the truce negotiations: quiescent when the talks were going badly, vituperative when an armistice appeared in sight. General Clark has described how his relations with Rhee were excellent "right up to the moment the United States indicated clearly it intended to go through with an armistice. . . . Then I became the whipping boy for his bitterness and frustration."[4]

As early as 1951, Rhee had set the pattern for his campaign to block any cease fire which would leave his country divided; he paid lip service to peace, but attached conditions to his acceptance of a cease fire which could not possibly be met. On June 30, 1951, Foreign Minister Pyun Yong-tae had announced that South Korea would accept a cease fire under the following conditions: withdrawal of all Chinese forces from North Korea; disarmament of North Korean armies; U.N. assurances that no "third power" would come to the aid of North Korea; a firm guarantee that the R.O.K. would participate in any international conference on the Korean problem; and an understanding that any arrangement that left Korea divided would have no legal effect.[5]

In the early spring of 1953, Rhee calculated how best to use his influence to block an armistice. From among Pyun's earlier "conditions" he chose as his opening wedge that which demanded a Chinese withdrawal from North Korea. On April 24, the R.O.K. ambassador in Washington informed the United States that South Korea would withdraw its forces from the U.N. Command if the Allies agreed to any armistice which permitted Chinese Communist troops to remain on Korean soil. Here, implicitly, was concrete evidence of Rhee's oft-repeated threats to march north. On instructions from Washington, General Clark hurried to Seoul to see Rhee lest he take any precipitate action. Rhee promised Clark nothing, but treated him to the sight of massed demonstrators calling for "unification or death."

In Panmunjom, meanwhile, implementation of Little Switch had not ended the stalemate on the issue of prisoner exchange. The U.N. position called for the release of all Korean nonrepatriates on the day of the armistice, allowing each freedom to settle in either the north or the south. Chinese nonrepatriates were to be turned over to a neutral commission for further "explanations" and ultimate disposition. The Communists, however, demanded that Koreans as well be turned over to neutral custody, and favored an "explanation period" of as long as nine months.

On May 11, the U.N. side recessed the negotiations once again.

Washington, finally at the limit of its patience, instructed Clark to agree to the Communist demand for a screening of all non-repatriates, but authorized him to break off negotiations if his counterproposal was not accepted or the Communists came up with a constructive alternative.

On May 25, the same day that the U.S. proposal was being presented to the Communists at Panmunjom, Clark and Ambassador Briggs called on Rhee and Foreign Minister Pyun in Seoul. Their task of selling Rhee on the subject of an armistice was not an enviable one; Rhee's most recent move had been to write Clark a letter rejecting any peace based upon a simultaneous withdrawal of U.N. and Communist forces from Korea. He now insisted upon a buffer zone north of the Yalu—a zone located in Chinese and Soviet territory—to be policed by the U.N. until permanent peace was established in the Far East. The fundamental opposition of the R.O.K. to *any* armistice was embodied in a statement by Pyun that South Korean troops would fire upon any Indian detachments sent to take custody of Communist prisoners.

Clark and Briggs, in their meeting with Rhee and Pyun, had an attractive package to sell. In return for Rhee's compliance with an armistice, and retention of the R.O.K. Army within the U.N. Command, the United States would build up the South Korean army to twenty divisions and would provide the equivalent of a billion dollars for the rehabilitation of South Korea. The sixteen nations participating in the U.N. Command, on their part, would announce that in the event of a new Communist attack they would return to the aid of the R.O.K., and might extend the war beyond the boundaries of Korea. But the Americans could have saved their breath. As General Clark has described the meeting:

"The emotional effect of this [exposition] on Rhee was profound. I had never seen him so disturbed. He sat bolt upright in his chair, the muscles of his face twitched occasionally and he kept rubbing the ends of his fingers. . . . Once he broke into our recital of our plans and promises and said:

" 'I am deeply disappointed. Your government changes its

position often. You pay no attention to the view of the ROK Government.'

"As it became increasingly clear that an armistice was a distinct probability and that Rhee's lifelong goal of an independent and undivided Korea had to be pushed into a future he might not live to see, the President became overwrought.

" 'One thing we must insist upon is the withdrawal of Chinese Communists from our territory,' he said. 'There can be no peaceful settlement without that. Your threats have no effect upon me. We want to live. We want to survive. We will decide our own fate.' "[6]

Anyone with knowledge of Rhee's negotiating techniques might have predicted his refusal of Clark's proposals. Rhee would certainly not agree to an armistice until he had played every card in his hand. In Washington, however, there appeared to be very little appreciation of the extent to which Rhee was capable of obstructing an armistice, or of his obvious willingness to do so. The United States, more accustomed to dealing with its European allies than with Asians, continued to treat South Korea as an equal, as a member of the Free World camp whose agreement with U.S. policies might be sought through bargaining but never through pressure. In practice, such classic diplomacy served only to sharpen Rhee's appetite. General Clark commented: "Behind all of Rhee's spoken and unspoken threats was the psychological whammy he had on us. He knew that no matter what happened we could not, after three years of war, after all the blood and treasure we lost, let Korea go to the Reds by default because of a quarrel 'in the family.' "[7]

On June 4, the U.N. and Communist sides reached agreement on all major points concerning prisoner repatriation. The Communists accepted the U.N.-proposed limit of three months for explanations to prisoners; the Allies agreed to drop their insistence on U.N. disposition of nonrepatriated prisoners in favor of direct resettlement by a neutral nations custodial commission. The South Korean press, which regularly publicized deliberate leaks from R.O.K. officials, denounced the agreement as a sellout. Rhee, on his part, attempted to muddy the waters once again: he would accept a truce based on the simultaneous withdrawal of *U.N. and Communist troops*, in return for a mutual security pact with the United States, large scale economic aid, and *the retention of U.S. air and naval forces in Korea.* R.O.K. officials privately admitted their awareness that these conditions would never be accepted by the Communists and that insistence on them only meant continuing the war.[8]

On June 7, Rhee underscored his threats of unilateral action by promulgating "extraordinary security measures" throughout South Korea, recalling R.O.K. Army officers from U.S. training schools, and by stepping up "march north" propaganda in domestic radio broadcasts. On the same day, ironically, General Clark conveyed to Rhee President Eisenhower's reply to South Korea's latest preconditions for an armistice. Eisenhower promised that following a truce in Korea the United States was prepared to negotiate a mutual defense treaty with South Korea. He reiterated previous promises of economic aid to the R.O.K. and promised that the United States would make Korean unification its "central objective" in the political conference which would follow an armistice. He emphasized, however, that the United States would disassociate itself from any march north.

Rhee immediately rejected Eisenhower's terms, calling upon the South Korean people to "reassert our determination to . . . fight on to a decisive end in case the U.N. accepts the truce and stops fighting." In view of Rhee's demonstrated penchant for attaching preconditions such as buffer zones and troop withdrawals to any cease fire, it was obvious that he was not seeking any workable arrangement. In his meetings with Clark, Rhee alternated between despair and defiance. He repeatedly accused the United States of appeasement, exclaiming on one occasion that "the Republic of Korea Army will fight on, if it means a suicide, and I will lead them."[9] Clark felt, however, that he had a commitment from Rhee that he would be informed before any action was taken to withdraw R.O.K. troops from the U.N. Command.

In Panmunjom, the rumblings from Seoul had gone largely unnoticed. If anything, the Communists must have been secretly pleased at Rhee's statements characterizing any armistice as a Communist victory. Neither the Communists nor the world at large felt that Rhee, on his own, could successfully obstruct an armistice. On June 8 came formal announcement from Panmunjom that agreement had been reached on the prisoner exchange issue. Then, on June 18, Rhee played his trump card: he ordered the release of all Communist prisoners who had refused repatriation. In the early morning hours South Korean guards opened the gates of prisoner enclosures, lit fires, and aided over 25,000 nonrepatriate prisoners to make their way into the Korean countryside. Announced Rhee:

"According to the Geneva Convention, and also to the principles of human rights, the anti-Communist Korean prisoners should have been released long before this. Most of the United Nations authorities with whom I have spoken about our desire to release these prisoners are with us in sympathy and principle. But due to the international complications we have been unjustly holding these people too long.

"In order to avoid the grave consequences which might result, I have ordered on my own responsibility the release of the anti-Communist Korean prisoners on this day, June 18, 1953.

"The reason why I did this without full consultation with the United Nations Command and other authorities concerned is too obvious to explain."[10]

The Communists, as Rhee doubtless hoped they would, broke off negotiations at Panmunjom, charging the United States with complicity in the escape. But the Free World reaction was hardly what Rhee had hoped. From everywhere came a stream of denunciation. Winston Churchill scored Rhee's "treachery" and stated flatly that the United Nations had no intention of conquering Korea on Rhee's behalf. Secretary Dulles told the South Korean ambassador that Rhee's action was "a stab in the back." Clark wrote to Rhee:

"I am profoundly shocked by this unilateral abrogation of your personal commitment. On several occasions in recent weeks you have personally assured both Ambassador Briggs and me that you would not take unilateral action with reference to ROK forces under my control until after full and frank discussion with me. Your actions today have clearly abrogated these assurances."[11]

What had Rhee expected to accomplish by this reckless action which drew such denunciations from his allies? How did the prisoner release fit into Rhee's hitherto skillful delaying tactics against the armistice?

The fact is that it did not fit in at all. The prisoner release appears to have been mainly the irresponsible act of a man who could no longer make logical judgments. Rhee, at seventy-eight years of age, was scarcely able to think beyond his overpowering ambition to unify Korea. He had lost touch with the world at large since his return to Korea in 1945, while coming to view the Korean problem as the overriding issue which faced the Free World. In his insistence on the vital importance of unification, he was supported not only by his own yes men but also by some Americans who found it easier to agree with the old gentleman than to disagree with him.

There is no particular evidence that Rhee actually expected the prisoner release to force his allies to fight the war through to a finish. While there was a possibility that the Communists might break off the negotiations and continue the war, the losses they had sustained in three years made this unlikely. In the absence of such action by the Communists there was no chance at all of the Allies stepping up the pace of the war. While Secretary Dulles was prepared to extend the war to Manchuria if the Communists failed to sign an armistice, he would have found little support in the United States for such a policy if the Communists had based a walk-out on a provocation like the prisoner release.

Basically, the prisoner release appears to have been less a calculated maneuver than a final act of defiance against an armistice which Rhee probably recognized as inevitable. For Rhee had other obstructionist tactics open to him which he did not use. With South Korean troops manning two-thirds of the battle line, he might have ordered a unilateral attack by R.O.K. Army troops. Although the threat of such a move would haunt the U.N. Command for some time to come, this was one step at which even Rhee drew the line. Although prone to talk in terms of "unification or death," Rhee had little interest in courses of action which offered no prospect of success.

The storm of criticism which greeted the prisoner release appeared to have an effect on Rhee, and his reply to Clark's letter was disjointed and dispirited in tone.

"As you say, I promised that I would let you know as a friend to a friend, when I have decided to withdraw our forces from the United Nations Command. That understanding still holds good. . . . The prisoners of war issue is, however, not to be confused with that. . . . .

"I would have consulted you beforehand, under ordinary circumstances, as I always did in any of the military measures. But now you know why I did not in this particular case. . . . If I did consult in advance, it would have been only an embarrassment to you. You may call it an act of violation on my part, but did the United Nations ever raise the question as to what the Communists ever did with our prisoners of war? We know what they did with them.

"To repeat what I said before, to release [the prisoners] as I did was the only way to avoid the danger of a clash between the Koreans and the foreign pro-communist troops you propose to bring in."*

Never one to stay long on the defensive, Rhee soon returned to

* R.O.K. Office of Public Information, *Korea Flaming High,* (Seoul, 1954–55), Vol. I, pp. 41–42. The "foreign pro-communist troops" were presumably the Indian custodial forces, later brought in to handle the repatriation of prisoners.

his charges of U.S. weakness in the face of communism. The United States, on its part, handed the initiative right back to Rhee. With Americans dying in a war that might have ended but for Rhee's action, Washington sent Assistant Secretary of State Walter Robertson to Seoul to "persuade" Rhee to accept an armistice. The old warrior, who thought that he had shot his bolt with the prisoner release, was not to be treated as a dangerous and unpredictable co-belligerent but as a respected ally. While General Clark set about answering Communist demands as to whether any meaningful armistice could be signed in view of Rhee's defiance, Rhee set about driving as hard a bargain as he could with his long-suffering benefactor.

At home in his mansion in Seoul, Rhee basked in the world spotlight as the American emissary, Robertson, sought to insure that he would not obstruct an armistice. It was a dramatic situation, one which Rhee could be counted upon to exploit to the utmost. The one bright spot was that while Rhee had repeatedly stated that he would not sign an armistice, he had indicated to Clark that he could "support" one.

For over two weeks Rhee and Robertson held bargaining sessions almost daily. Like the American negotiators at Panmunjom, Robertson was forced to listen to streams of vituperation against the United States. Like the Communists, Rhee time and time again interjected new conditions into the acceptance of any truce. It was not that he and Robertson were far apart in terms of what South Korea might receive in return for a cease fire; indeed, Rhee conceded at the outset that the American package proposal met most of his demands. The Korean, however, would put nothing in writing so long as he thought there might be further concessions to be gained. "The record of the talks," observed General Clark, "showed that the U.S. leaned over backwards to meet almost all of Rhee's demands, only to have him throw in a few new ones."[12] Once more in control of the emotions that had prompted the prisoner release, Rhee was again the wily horse trader.

Outside the negotiating room, Rhee created a background suit-

11. The Revolt of April 1960: A tense moment in Seoul as demonstrating students and other citizens confront the regime's military forces. This was on April 19, when violent uprisings rocked the Rhee government and the aged leader called out the army to impose martial law. (*Wide World Photo*)

able for the occasion. Seoul was covered with banners and placards attacking the armistice, most of them in English. Each day as Robertson drove to the presidential mansion he was treated to anti-armistice demonstrations in the streets. The *New York Times* reported:

"A strange emotional mass demonstration was put on by teen-age girls of Seoul High School yesterday afternoon.

"About 500 students in white middy blouses and blue skirts appeared just before 1 P.M. at the crest of a hill about a half-mile east of the Capitol Building. At a signal from their leaders they broke into a run in formation, eight abreast, and continued down the main avenue past the burned-out Capitol. They continued until they reached the correspondents' billet about a quarter mile farther on. At the barred gate they clustered in a semi-circle and sat on the ground.

"One of the older girls raised her hand and in response the nearly exhausted children drew white handkerchiefs from their blouses and began to sob. As the sobs grew louder tears appeared, and mass hysteria swept through the crowd.

"The girls leaped to their feet shrieking and waving their arms. One girl fainted and was pulled to safety from the crowd. Others fell under the sea of waving white.

"The demonstration continued slightly less than an hour."[13]

The "little truce talks" ended anticlimactically on July 12 when Robertson flew to Tokyo with a letter from Rhee to Eisenhower agreeing not to obstruct an armistice. In Tokyo and in Washington, Robertson met with congratulations for a job well done—a task of persuasion which in most governments of the world would never have arisen. In Seoul, Rhee beat his breast, emphasizing the reluctance with which South Korea was even concurring in an armistice. But as an old bargainer, he must have recognized that his accomplishments were impressive.

Rhee's letter to Eisenhower agreeing to a cease fire was his only substantive concession. Even here Rhee's agreement was qualified: he reserved the right to withdraw from the post-armistice political conference and take any action he deemed necessary if he was dissatisfied with its progress after ninety days. In return for this, Rhee obtained:

1. The promise of a R.O.K.—U.S. mutual security treaty after the armistice took effect;
2. A lump payment of $200,000,000, plus ten million pounds of food, as the first installment of a long-term aid program;
3. An agreement that both the U.S. and the R.O.K. would withdraw from the political conference after ninety days if there should be no concrete moves towards Korean unification within that time;
4. Expansion of the R.O.K. Army to twenty divisions, and a modest expansion of the navy and air force;
5. Agreement to confer on common R.O.K.—U.S. objectives before the opening of the post-armistice conference.

The agreement was a triumph for Rhee. If it did not guarantee Korean unification, it nonetheless embodied promises which Rhee had sought for years: the protection afforded by a mutual defense treaty with a great power, coupled with a commitment that he would be consulted on all matters affecting Korea. On top of this there was the prospect of large-scale economic aid for his country.

On July 27, one of history's dirtiest, most vicious, and most frustrating wars came to a close with the signing of an armistice at Panmunjom. Now there remained only the physical exchange of prisoners and the implementation of the complex truce mechanism. Those who knew Rhee best assumed correctly that he would make every effort to harass both of these procedures. But throughout the Free World there was at least relief that the shooting had stopped.

With the signing of the armistice Rhee regained abroad a little of his status as a redoubtable old warrior who had fought the Communists so hard for so long. If it was too early for dispassionate comment concerning Rhee's skill as a negotiator, the Free World in general was sympathetic to the president's desire for unification. But persons close to the scene were less inclined to be charitable. General Clark observed:

"I don't think there is much point in totting up who got the best of the [Rhee-Robertson] bargain. The most that can be said is that the talks proved to the world that South Korea was no puppet state. No doubt we saved Rhee much face in handling him the way we did. . . .

"[But] we lost more than face. We lost lives. The war at that time was costing us an average of nine hundred United Nations casualties a day and the maddening part of it was that we had been in complete agreement with the Communists on the truce terms and were down to talk about the signing ceremony when the prisoners were released."[14]

13: Keeping the Pot Boiling

WHILE he held the world spotlight with his anti-armistice activity during 1953, Rhee kept a characteristically close watch on the domestic political scene. For one of his years, he had a remarkable ability to follow events in several different areas at the same time. Just as he had waged his antiarmistice campaign at the same time as he fought the National Assembly in 1952, he thought little of precipitating a minor political crisis in the midst of the furor which attended the prisoner release the following year.

To the surprise of Lee Bum-suk, Rhee now made it clear that he regarded him as a bit of unfinished business left over from the 1952 election. Rhee, by his eleventh-hour support of Ham Tai-yong in the vice-presidential election, had defeated Lee's bid to entrench himself as Rhee's political lieutenant and probable heir. But even after this check to Lee's ambitions the president was not satisfied. While he was incensed that Lee had claimed to be Rhee's own choice for the vice-presidency, he was also concerned at the effectiveness of the strong-arm machine Lee had made of his Racial Youth Corps. Lee's success in browbeating the Assembly had made a deep impression on Rhee, but not entirely as Lee had hoped. Never one to let gratitude interfere with practical politics, Rhee was impressed with the fact that Lee's control of the R.Y.C. gave him a larger following than he had allowed anyone before Lee.

The result was that an empire fell in a day. Rhee found Lee's absence from Korea on a tour of the United States an opportune time for wielding the axe. During the war years Lee had planted his adherents throughout the cabinet, the police, and the Liberal Party. Within a matter of days, however, Rhee accomplished a purge so sweeping that it recalled the government by edict of some of the Yi dynasty kings.

Once Rhee had knocked the props from under Lee, there was no shortage of politicians to finish the job. As successor to Lee in the premiership, Rhee chose Chang Taik-sang, whose efforts on the president's behalf in the Assembly crisis had been a good deal more sophisticated than Lee's. To purge the Liberal Party organization of pro-Youth Corps elements Rhee chose Lee Ki-bung, a one-time minister of defense who had not even supported the administration during the election period. At the time of their appointments, neither man was felt to have greatly improved his political prospects. Rhee, it was felt, would use them to clean up the administration until criticism mounted, and then would show them the door. But if this was to be Chang's fate, it was not the case with Lee Ki-bung. Lee, whose prospects in 1953 seemed even less promising than Chang's, was fated to stay on as Rhee's political man Friday until he was eventually recognized as Rhee's choice as his successor.

At first glance Rhee appeared to have cut Lee Bum-suk down to size in much the same manner as he had operated on the likes of Cho Byong-ok, Cho Bong-am, and others who he feared were acquiring too much power. But Rhee's appointment of Lee Ki-bung, a political moderate, to succeed Lee Bum-suk as boss of the Liberal Party suggested that Rhee desired to disassociate himself from some of the excesses of 1952. As a professed democrat, Rhee may have been embarrassed at some of the methods employed on his behalf, especially in the light of the criticism they had brought on his government and himself.

In any case, Lee Ki-bung, a reasonably efficient administrator with no pretensions to brilliance or leadership, was almost the antithesis of his martial predecessor. Rhee would come to rely on the unassuming Lee even after the 1956 election had demonstrated that his very moderation almost brought about the downfall of the Liberal Party. In retrospect, however, Rhee's choice of Lee Ki-bung to head the Liberal Party represented, in a modest way, a trend away from the blatant strong-arm methods of 1952.

A past master at playing one personality against another, Rhee handled the domestic political scene without seeming effort after 1952. Following the Racial Youth Corps purge he returned to efforts to nullify the armistice. Fearful that with the cease fire an accomplished fact the world might forget Korea, Rhee periodically put the R.O.K. Army on alert, or dropped a carefully-timed reminder that South Korea was not a signatory to the armistice. The fact that Rhee's specific agreement not to obstruct the armistice applied for only ninety days caused apprehension concerning his course of action in the likely event that agreement on Korean unification was not reached in East-West negotiations in Geneva.

The autumn of 1953 brought the prisoner exchange which had been awaited through literally years of debate at Panmunjom. Rhee, however, was as adept at impeding implementation of the armistice as he was in attacking it in principle. Petulantly, he refused to allow Indian troops—which under the terms of the armistice were to administer the explanations and prisoner exchange—to set foot on South Korean soil. He insisted that this was not a violation of his pledge not to obstruct the armistice. Nonetheless, the U.S. Army eventually had to fly the Indians by helicopter from ships to the neutral demilitarized zone. As time went on, the Indians became second only to the Japanese as Rhee's favorite Free World whipping boys.

If the clouds had any silver lining for Syngman Rhee, it was the signing, on August 8, 1953, of a mutual security treaty between the R.O.K. and the United States. Here was the culmination of a lifelong ambition, an event which allowed a bitter old man to recall with some satisfaction how, nearly fifty years ago, he had traveled to the United States to plead in vain for American protection against the Japanese. Rhee made the signing the occasion for a discourse on Korean history:

"Korea has been considered as a weak, minor country, helplessly situated among powerful nations and yet rich in natural resources, thereby attracting many an aggressive power to covet the land. Throughout history Korea has been regarded as a 'no-man's land' whose independence, neighboring powers assumed, is unavoidably dependent on one of the big powers. . . . This unfortunately resulted in the conquest of Korea by militaristic Japan, which, with the aid of the Western world, subjugated us into forty years of dishonorable and abject slavery, unprecedented in our long history. Following Japan's failure to conquer the whole world, the Allied nations brought up a decision made by themselves [which] finally caused the tragic division of Korea, north and south.

"Nevertheless, the united effort of our people, the patriotism of our youth, and the assistance from friendly nations, all contributed to developing our armed forces, within a remarkably short period of time, into a strong military power—indeed, one of the most powerful forces in Asia. Now that a defense treaty has been signed between Korea and the United States our posterity will enjoy the benefits accruing from the treaty for generations to come. Our united effort in this field will assure our security, protecting us from alien aggressors."[1]

Most of the time, however, Rhee's speeches were devoted to giving the Americans fits with his threats of a march north. It was difficult to discount Rhee's sabre-rattling; he so obviously desired to go down in the history books as the George Washington of Korea, and had so dramatically demonstrated his impetuosity when crossed, that it was years after the armistice before American military commanders were able to discount the possibility of an abortive R.O.K. attack. Here as elsewhere, Rhee viewed himself as a spokesman for the whole Korean people. But although the

12. The Revolt of April 1960: Demonstrating students dive to the ground as police open fire on them. Other students (left) flee from the shooting. The date was April 19. (*Wide World Photo*)

Korean people genuinely desired the unification of their country, there was evidence everywhere that they had had enough of fighting. With most of the country at a near-starvation level, and with disease rampant and inflation sweeping the country, South Korea was ready for peace.

To Rhee, however, whose material wants were looked after and to whom, in any case, abstractions had a way of seeming more real than realities, peace without unification was anathema. He was only vaguely sympathetic toward his people's privations; had he not been tortured for his own work in the original Independence Club? Rhee's fires burned deep, and it was a measure of his belief as well as his oratory that he communicated his feelings to his audiences as he did. However initially apathetic were the wretched Seoulites whom the police turned out to hear their president, few remained unmoved after Rhee shuffled to the microphone to describe the plight of their brethren in the north. His eyes were watery and often half closed. His hands shook. But as his whispered words grew stronger, appealing to his countrymen for patriotism and self-sacrifice, Rhee left some observers with an uneasy feeling that he might indeed spark a new war with the sound of his own voice.

The Geneva conference on the Far East opened on April 26, 1954, with Rhee's shrill threats of a march north as background. Taking part were the foreign ministers of nineteen countries: those of the sixteen-nation U.N. Command, plus the U.S.S.R., Communist China, and North Korea. For Rhee, this was the political conference on Korean unification for which the armistice agreement had provided. For the record, it was the last time (up to the present date) that R.O.K. and North Korean representatives were to meet around a conference table. But the Geneva conference had on its agenda the Indochina question as well as that of Korea, and many observers felt that the former area held out the better prospects for compromise.

On the Korean issue, Communist and non-Communist delegates

alike paid lip service to the concept of a unified, independent Korea, but East and West stood poles apart on how to achieve it. Representing the R.O.K., Foreign Minister Pyun Yong-tae proposed that U.N.-supervised elections be held in North Korea for the hundred-odd seats in the R.O.K. Assembly being held open for North Korean legislators. For the north, Foreign Minister Nam Il, choosing not to recognize the geographical realities which would permit Chinese troops to return to Korea in a matter of days, proposed that all foreign troops be withdrawn from Korea. However much Rhee had been attracted by this concept at various times, it was now unacceptable if only because it was a Communist proposal. Also unworkable was a vague Communist proposal calling for all-Korea elections supervised by a commission composed of North Korean and R.O.K. legislators. With neither side prepared to compromise, the conference degenerated into a stalemate.

On May 22, a Western counterproposal calling for U.N. supervision of all-Korea elections was agreed to by the R.O.K., which previously had rejected the concept of all-Korea elections on the grounds that elections supervised by the United Nations had already been held in South Korea. But this concession was followed by a demand by Pyun that Chinese forces be withdrawn from North Korea before any elections were held. Since the Communists were scarcely willing to agree to any U.N.-supervised elections—in effect, supervision by one belligerent—the impasse was only deepened. With both sides setting forth proposals largely for propaganda effect, no real settlement was in prospect.[2]

After seven weeks of stalemate, the negotiations broke down amid mutual recriminations. Neither side had shown a willingness to make any substantial concessions on the Korean issue, and what positive results came from Geneva concerned only Indochina. Syngman Rhee, however, had achieved another goal that dated back to his days in the Independence Club: South Korea was being treated as an equal in discussions of the Korean problem by the great powers of the world. Superficially at least, Korea was no longer being handled as a Poland of the Far East, a land to be divided and distributed at the whims of the great powers.

In retrospect, however, R.O.K. diplomacy at Geneva was scarcely that of a nation seeking unification at any price. For all Rhee's oratory concerning Korea's inability to exist divided, he showed little inclination to gamble on his nation's ability to resist subversion from the north and to seek a workable formula for the supervision of all-Korea elections. While it is problematical whether any arrangement would have satisfied both East and West, it nonetheless became apparent at Geneva that South Korea was more disposed to accept the *status quo* than to negotiate with the Communists on terms other than those laid down by Rhee.

Back in Seoul, Rhee seized on the failure at Geneva as new evidence that unification could never be achieved except by force. Rhee's denunciations of his erstwhile allies became strident as he came to view the Korean War almost exclusively in terms of its failure to unify Korea under his regime:

"Let us not forget that the war was fought for the purpose of bringing about a united, independent and democratic Korea. That purpose cannot be ignored, forgotten, or pushed out of consciousness; it remains the constant objective of the Republic of Korea in peace or war. But let me say this, in fairness to all: if there are any nations or any fighting men in Korea who do not believe that the battle has anything to do with the defense of their own peace and security, then let them go home. We do not want them to shed their blood for a cause in which they do not believe, for a cause they do not think is theirs."[3]

Most of Rhee's generals, however, knew better than he the hopelessness of a march north. In the year which had followed the armistice both sides had developed impressive defenses in depth. The R.O.K. Army, which had been taking it on the chin from the Chinese in the final months of the war, could scarcely stand a chance in any solo attack against its well-entrenched enemy. The Communist bloc had failed in its attempts to destroy the R.O.K., first by subversion and then by war. But with no political settlement in sight, the two sides settled down to watch each other in an uneasy truce which finally came to be an accepted part of the Far Eastern scene.

On both sides of the demarcation line, the staggering work of reconstruction began. On neither side, however, was the lot of the impoverished man-in-the-street a matter of much concern. In North Korea, where the devastation was perhaps even greater than in the South, the Communists gave first priority to the reconstruction of heavy industries such as steel and electric power —items in demand in both China and the U.S.S.R.—despite appalling shortages of agricultural and consumer goods. In South Korea, a combination of corruption, administrative inefficiency, and sheer obstructionism delayed the International Cooperation Administration program for months. The main bottleneck, however, was Rhee himself. The functioning of the South Korean government was such that all except the most minor decisions were referred to Rhee, and the result was confusion compounded. One correspondent wrote in December 1953:

"The United States has pledged one billion dollars for [Korean] reconstruction. But the program is not yet underway, except in a token sense, because the Rhee Government has delayed in giving assurances on several basic matters. Such agreement from other governments would be considered routine. . . .

"Official visits to Dr. Rhee's home are an almost daily ritual. Usually the President has been cordial and appeared to be cooperative. At some point, however, usually at the end of negotiations, there is apt to be a reversal, and the diplomat finds himself back where he started.

"Sometimes Dr. Rhee is not cooperative at all. At one recent talk he never got to the substance of the discussion but complained about Americans in general and the draftiness of the plane lent to him by the United States to carry him to a meeting with Generalissimo Chiang Kai-shek on Formosa. . . .

"During negotiations the Rhee Government has behaved in a way that caused one diplomat to remark that 'they are unquestionably the most difficult people with whom I have ever had to deal.' "[4]

It was the misfortune of the South Korean people to be ruled by an embittered septuagenarian whose personal shortcomings were compounded by his being surrounded by inept and often corrupt subordinates. Thus Liberal Party politicos were able to assure the rehabilitation of their bombed-out property holdings; businessmen bribed administration officials to obtain reconstruction contracts; and police officials supervised the motley gangs of sneak thieves which pillaged each new load of relief goods on the docks at Pusan. But as the rich got richer and the poor stayed poor, Rhee once again turned his attention to international affairs.

14: Rhee and Japan

FOR ALL his renown as a foe of communism, a compilation of Rhee's speeches as president of South Korea would probably reveal that the greatest target of his invective was not the Communists but the Japanese. Rhee felt no need to warn his own people against communism; no one knew its dangers better than they. He did feel a need to warn the world against neutral governments such as those of India, Indonesia, and Burma, which he regarded as pro-Communist and scarcely better than the bloc nations themselves. But his greatest invective was reserved for Japan, which in his view was the most dangerous of the "neutralists" in its ability to delude the United States as to its true motives. "To her erstwhile major enemy," observed Rhee, "Japan has turned a Machiavellian face that is deceiving the guileless Americans."[1] New antagonists in no way dulled the edge of Rhee's hatred of Japan, and even while he fought the Communists to the north he inveighed against the enemy to the east. Far from supporting the American effort to democratize Japan, Rhee charged categorically that Japan was planning a new invasion of Korea, and even during the Korean War labored strenuously to exclude Japan as a source of war materiel for the U.N. forces.

Rhee's attitude toward Japan was understandable in one who had fought that country all his life and who was capable of strong hatreds. Yet in contrast to many of his dealings with the United States, where his obstinacy paid off handsomely in terms of commitments from the United States, Rhee's war against Japan was a barren vendetta which served to retard South Korea's recovery from the war without having any real effect on Japan. The Rhee government might have enjoyed a flourishing postwar trade with Japan, exchanging the Korean rice favored by the Japanese for industrial goods and machinery. But Rhee would have none of this, and all but prohibited commerce between Japan and Korea. Perhaps it was asking too much for the aging Rhee to forget his life-long battle against the Japanese. Nonetheless, on no other issue did Rhee's emotionalism carry him further away from the best interests of his country, for the existence of Japan was not something which Rhee could wish away.

In keeping alive the historical antagonism between Korea and its neighbor, Rhee developed an impressive list of grievances against the Japanese. Some went back to before World War II: Rhee demanded the return, even from private collectors, of Korean art objects bought or confiscated during the occupation. He demanded cash repayment for Korean natural resources exploited by the Japanese. He refused, however, to consider compensation for Japanese citizens whose property in Korea was confiscated after liberation.

On top of such problems stemming from the Japanese occupation came new irritants in the post-liberation period. Following the surrender of Japan, some two million Koreans, many of whom had been used for forced labor in Japan, were repatriated to Korea. But a half a million others elected to stay in Japan even though they were treated as social inferiors. The Japanese would have liked to repatriate these too, but because they were largely leftist in sympathy, and often had criminal records, the R.O.K. would neither accept them nor permit them to select repatriation to North Korea.

Issues such as reparations and the status of Korean residents in Japan were problems which almost inevitably must have caused friction between Japan and her former colony. But far from attempting to resolve differences, Rhee sought to compound them by a deliberate policy of encouraging anti-Japanese sentiment in the Korean populace. And far from acknowledging the importance of Japan as a staging area for the U.N. Command, Rhee made the wartime period—when he felt most assured of U.S. support—the period of his most flagrant harassment of Japan.

Following the outbreak of the Korean War, General MacArthur had proclaimed a maritime security area around the Korean peninsula from which most categories of neutral shipping, including Japanese fishing craft, were excluded. The armistice subsequently prohibited sea blockades, however, and in August 1953 the Sea Defense Zone was suspended by General Clark. The R.O.K. reaction was violent. A government spokeman announced:

"We have always regarded General Clark as highly competent and a responsible commander. It is therefore, ironical and regrettable that now, near the conclusion of his major mission against communism, he should be unaware of what a valuable present large areas of unguarded seas can be to the enemy. . . .

"The Republic of Korea will, of course, for protection of itself and its friends, continue to enforce the peace line proclaimed by President Rhee."[2]

The "peace line," which shortly became known as the Rhee line, ultimately came to encompass even more of the high seas than had the area originally delineated by General MacArthur. And it soon became obvious that the target of the Rhee line was not the Communists, but the Japanese. Fishing boats which ventured across the Rhee line were seized by the Koreans, usually with patrol craft provided by the United States. Not only were the boats seized, but the offending fishermen were jailed in Korean prisons, and often remained incarcerated even after serving their sentences. Seizures of Japanese craft on the high seas in 1953 gave the final year of the Korean War the aspect of a two-front war.

Equally typical of Rhee's nose-thumbing towards the Japanese was the case of the Liancourt Rocks. These barren islands, located halfway between Japan and Korea, were claimed by both countries though occupied by neither. Rhee was incensed, however, when U.N. aircraft used the islands in 1952 for a bombing range without requesting his permission. The R.O.K. formally protested to the U.N. Command and moved to station a force on the islands. With an air of having defeated both the U.N. Command and the Japanese, Rhee garrisoned the islands and used them as an outpost from which to snipe at Japanese fishing boats.

During the period of the armistice negotiations Rhee appeared to go to any lengths to humiliate the Japanese. Like the Indians, the Japanese were prohibited from landing on Korean soil. Japanese technicians, a number of whom were in the employ of the U.S. Navy at Inchon, had to be escorted when there was business ashore lest they be arrested by R.O.K. police. When the armistice was signed, Rhee refused to allow Japanese newsmen to attend the ceremony, even though South Korea was not a signatory to the armistice.

Among American officialdom in Korea it became fashionable to debate whether Rhee hated the Japanese more than the Communists, or vice versa. It is doubtful, however, whether Rhee himself indulged in such fancies. He knew that he was able to get a sympathetic hearing concerning his objections to an armistice, because the Americans had no more delusions than he about Communist good faith. But Rhee felt himself alone in his warnings against Japanese duplicity. Having thus cast himself in the role of a voice crying in the wilderness, Rhee filled the pages of the government press with abuse of the Japanese, and made the Rhee line a cornerstone of R.O.K. foreign policy.

The upshot was that in a period from 1952 through 1955 the Japanese lost several hundred ships to the South Koreans. To add insult to injury, the R.O.K. refused to repatriate Japanese fishermen who had completed their sentences; these were kept under confinement in internment camps in protest against alleged Japanese mistreatment of Koreans in Japan. Postwar Japanese governments, surprisingly enough, showed great restraint in their relations with the Rhee government. Anxious for the world to forget its past sins, Tokyo accepted each new insult from Seoul with such humility that Japan's inability to protect its fishermen became an issue in Japanese domestic politics.

With the United States in effect an embarrassed middleman in Rhee's campaign against the Japanese, it was virtually inevitable that Washington should end up in the role of mediator between its erstwhile enemy and its new, troublesome ward. Rhee, for his part, recognized U.S. hopes for improved R.O.K.-Japanese relations as susceptible to manipulation. He soon discovered that he could please the Americans merely by an occasional diminishing of anti-Japanese propaganda, at no cost to himself. In late 1952, after suitable cajoling from Washington, Rhee even entered into negotiations in Tokyo aimed at "normalizing" relations between Japan and Korea. A Korean mission was accredited to Tokyo, even though the R.O.K. permitted no Japanese diplomatic establishment in Seoul.

With issues such as reparations claims, the Rhee line, and the question of Korean residents in Japan facing the negotiators, prospects for success were dubious at best. The demands of the R.O.K. delegation were such, however, that the talks never really got off the ground. So extravagant were Korean claims against the Japanese occupation that the Japanese felt compelled to put forth a modest bill of their own for Japanese property confiscated by the Koreans after 1945. Subsequent discussion of the reparations issue brought a remark from a Japanese delegate that his country's occupation of Korea had not been entirely without benefit to the Koreans. Although the Japanese government later disavowed the remark, Rhee characterized it as an insult to R.O.K. sovereignty and broke off the talks.

Rhee's animosity towards the Japanese did more than keep alive old hatreds; it was an element in the North Asian scene which worked actively to the advantage of the Communists. Ship seizures by the South Koreans encouraged anti-American feeling among the Japanese, who, like the Communists, could not believe that Rhee could take actions which were actively opposed by the United States. In addition, Rhee's anti-Japanese vendetta effectively precluded any anti-Communist alliance in North Asia, emphasizing instead an area of discord within the Free World.

In early 1954, Rhee realized a long-cherished ambition with the inauguration—at South Korea's behest—of the Asian People's Anti-Communist League, a loose grouping of delegations from Free World areas such as Korea, Formosa, Hong Kong, and the Philippines. The first meeting was held at Rhee's vacation resort, Chinhae, near Pusan.

Although it did little except pass strongly worded resolutions, there was something to be said for the league as a step in the direction of an anti-Communist alliance. Indeed, an alliance of South Korea, Formosa, and Japan would have represented a very real military potential backed by the heavy industry of Japan. But Rhee's attitude towards Japan precluded Tokyo's participating in any grouping which included South Korea; in fact, it soon became apparent that a major function of the league, in Rhee's view, was to alert his fellow Asians against the menace of resurgent Japan. Proposals that Japan be admitted to the league were vigorously opposed by the R.O.K., and the Asian People's Anti-Communist League gradually withered on the vine.

South Korea and Nationalist China, in the postwar period, displayed entirely different attitudes towards their former enemy, Japan. Although not even the Koreans suffered more at the hands of the Japanese than did the Chinese, old antagonisms did not prevent Chiang Kai-shek from building up a flourishing trade between Formosa and Japan, thus making commercial considerations an effective check against domestic pressures for the reçognition of Communist China. Alone in Asia, Syngman Rhee pursued a policy of attempting to isolate Japan from the Free World. He scorned the Nationalist policy of friendship towards Japan, and was able to do so because American aid made him less dependent on the Japanese economy. But he spoke as though for all his fellow-Asians:

"When Americans say their beneficent occupation changed the Japanese, people in Asia shake their heads negatively. . . . [Japan] retains her arrogant and domineering attitude in her relations with other Asians.

"Nevertheless, the United States is following a policy to restore Japan to status as the leading country in the Orient, economically, politically, and militarily, in that order, though there is little lag between the three spheres. An industrial nation's ramifications are limitless. As the producing nation, Japan would crack the whip. Her neighbors, as customers, would be dependent upon her for every critical item and helpless at her whim. . . .

"I can say with confidence that 400 million Chinese would rather remain under Communism's bonds than to fight their way to freedom only to be forced by America into slavery again under the Japanese."[3]

For years relations between South Korea and Japan continued frigid. Most vexing to the Japanese were the continued seizure of their fishing craft and Rhee's unwillingness to agree to the repatriation of Koreans in Japan to either North or South Korea. Armed clashes sometimes took place when Japanese fishermen attempted to escape Rhee's patrol boats. Yet when R.O.K.-Japanese relations came to a head, the crisis was triggered not by the Rhee line but by the seemingly less pressing issue of repatriation.

In December 1958, Rhee had offered to return to Japan those fishermen who were being detained in Korea even after they had completed prison tours for violations of the Rhee line. This humane gesture was accompanied by an offer to resume the formal talks concerning "normalization" which had been broken off by the R.O.K. in 1953.

In Japan, however, pressures were building up concerning the repatriation of Korean residents. North Korea, which was feeling the effects of an acute manpower shortage left over from the war, redoubled its efforts to obtain immigrants from Japan. Sentiment among Koreans in Japan—who knew little of North Korea but who had heard all too much about life in the South—was favorable towards repatriation to Communist Korea. The Japanese government, which asked only to be rid of as many Koreans as possible, gingerly requested the International Red Cross to screen those Koreans who indicated that they desired to go to North Korea.

Despite shrill protests from Rhee, the Kishi government proceeded with its plans for repatriation during 1959. Once again Seoul broke off its "normalization" negotiations, and Rhee hinted that he would attempt to intercept any repatriation ship bound for a North Korean port. But in December the exodus began.

The publicity which has attended the repatriation to North Korea does not compare with that accorded the hundreds of thousands of North Koreans who moved south to escape the Communists during the Korean War. But its implications to the Free World are serious. For the first time during the cold war, persons living in the Free World have chosen in large numbers to live under communism instead. By mid-May 1960, nearly twenty thousand Koreans had left Japan for North Korea aboard Soviet ships, and the flow showed no signs of abating. Few of the repatriates had family ties in North Korea, and the more intelligent ones recognized that they faced an uncertain future. But all were weary of their poverty-stricken existence in an alien land, and had found their way to South Korea blocked by Syngman Rhee.

15: Rhee and Washington

PEACE came uneasily to South Korea. To its people—there were twenty-two million of them crowded into the southern half of the peninsula—the armistice came none too soon; by 1953, patriotism had been subordinated to a day-to-day scramble for the bare necessities of existence, and continued talk of new war did nothing except keep nerves on edge. It was one thing to fight a liberation war. It was another thing to be left with so uncertain a peace that no one could be sure whether it was really peace or merely a brief respite.

Syngman Rhee had proved an able war leader. Most of his severest critics agreed that he had rallied his people to fight the Communists as perhaps no one else could have done. And if the war had ended with his country still divided, the situation could hardly be blamed on Rhee. Unfortunately for all concerned, his allies viewed the armistice with satisfaction and an air of finality; Rhee not only opposed it, but was constitutionally incapable of accepting it. Far from counting his blessings and attempting to guide his country through the period of reconstruction, Rhee aimed squarely for the unattainable. Not only did he not feel gratitude for South Korea's survival; he blamed America and her allies for stopping short of the total victory which would have established him as president of a united Korea. Complained Rhee:

"We hope that [our allies] may soon come to understand that the only way to protect their own liberties is by undertaking once again to join in a common front to push the aggressor back from the free territory he has seized. We hope that they may see that through boldness in fighting for our just rights is the only path to final world peace."

Rhee chose to ignore the fact that the aggressor had indeed been thrown back and that South Korea occupied more of Korea after the armistice than in 1950. He seemed to forget that countries with no immediate interest in the fate of the remote Korean peninsula had come to his aid in the fighting and had at least restored the prewar *status quo*. Rhee rambled on:

"But if they do not join with us, we shall have to go forward alone. Free men everywhere are with us in their hearts and with their good will. The cause for which we fight is the cause of civilization itself. We will not falter and in the final analysis we cannot fail."[1]

Shorn of their rhetoric, Rhee's threats nonetheless made it clear that as far as he, Syngman Rhee, was concerned, the war was not over. As a result, it was years before South Korea began to behave like a country in a reconstruction period. No one dared undertake any permanent construction, lest Rhee launch an attack which would once again bring devastation from the north. The government frowned upon the introduction of consumer goods into a country on a wartime footing, and as a result inflation continued in a dizzy spiral.

Notwithstanding Rhee's attitude, the Free World responded generously to the challenge of Korean reconstruction. The United Nations participated through the United Nations Korean Reconstruction Agency, one of the more successful programs. Missionary organizations supported hospitals and schools. The Eighth U.S. Army, under its Armed Forces Aid to Korea program, provided building materials and technical advice for projects built by Korean labor. Finally the I.C.A., which had millions of dollars to spend, thanks to Rhee's skillful bargaining during the armistice negotiations, loomed on the scene. Even with the most willing hands, however, the prospect was appalling. Almost totally devastated by the war, South Korea had virtually no natural re-

13. The Revolt of April 1960: Families of riot victims grieve during a ceremony for the dead held in Seoul. (*Wide World Photo*)

sources or electric power and had become a rice-deficit area under the strain of supporting millions of refugees from the north.

In the rehabilitation of Korea as in the fighting, the United States carried the lion's share of the load. The I.C.A. went about its task in the time-honored manner of bureaucracies: fact-finding teams, five-year plans, symbolic cornerstone layings, and large scale industrial projects. No one, least of all Syngman Rhee, heeded the fact that for centuries Korea had operated on the basis of agricultural and cottage industry and had none of the prerequisites for an industrial power. But industrialization was the watchword, and U.S. funds constructed many a factory which was subsequently turned over to Liberal Party businessmen whose donations continued to keep the Rhee administration in office.

Whatever the shortcomings of the U.S. aid program, Washington quickly recognized the need of checking the inflation which was rapidly making the South Korean *hwan* all but worthless. The antidote to inflation: importation of sufficient consumer goods to supply the immediate wants of the people, and to soak up enough of the currency in circulation to establish the hwan at a realistic rate in terms of the goods it would buy. However sensible this concept, it ran into vehement opposition from Rhee. Not only was Rhee loath to subordinate industrialization to the importation of perishables, but he had his own ideas on the cause and cure of inflation. While acknowledging that the shortage of consumer goods was a contributing factor, Rhee attributed spiraling prices chiefly to the insistence of the U.N. Command on devaluing the hwan every few months in accordance with its decreasing purchasing power. It was useless to argue that the hwan-dollar exchange rate merely reflected South Korea's inflationary trend; Rhee insisted that devaluation caused inflation, and demanded a permanently fixed exchange rate which, to the surprise of no one, he wished established at a rate which grossly overvalued the hwan.

During the first half of 1954, the value of the hwan plummeted from 15–1 to 180–1. Even this latter figure was surpassed, though out of deference to Rhee's sensibilities the U.N. Command continued to purchase hwan at 180–1. In May, however, the U.N. Command finally discontinued purchases of hwan until such a time as it was pegged at a realistic rate. Rhee in turn promptly suspended hwan advances to the U.N. Command, and in so doing ignored a previous commitment that the R.O.K. would continue to advance hwan until a mutually acceptable settlement could be reached. Korean employees of the U.N. forces, at best scarcely able to live from day to day, went without wages.

Ultimately, Rhee had things pretty much his own way. In November, Rhee obtained a fixed exchange rate pegged at 500–1, even though by then the black market rate was over 800–1. No one on the U.N. side was particularly happy about the arrangement, except that it held some promise of disposing of the exchange-rate dispute for the time being. The affair is of interest, however, if only because it demonstrated Rhee's *modus operandi*. He could be so unpleasant to deal with, and was so prone to attack his allies' motives when crossed, that on any except the most vital issues his American colleagues preferred to let him have his way and hope for the best.

As time went on, Rhee's frustrations at the continued division of his country more and more frequently manifested themselves in attacks against the United States. The government press regularly attacked the armistice, insinuating that the United States was duped into signing it. Although by 1954 the armistice was taking on a more or less permanent aspect, Rhee remained no less anxious to demonstrate his opposition to it at every opportunity.

For two years after the armistice, inspection teams comprising representatives of Sweden, Switzerland, Czechoslovakia, and Poland had "enforced" the armistice on both sides of the demilitarized zone, particularly with respect to the introduction of new weapons. In North Korea the inspection was a fiasco, as the Swiss and Swedes were flagrantly barred from inspecting those areas into which the Communists were introducing new equipment. It was the U.N. Command's scrupulous observance of the armistice terms—which allowed the Czech and Pole inspectors to travel freely in South Korea—that aroused Rhee's ire. In 1954 and again in the following year, the R.O.K. initiated "spontaneous" demonstrations against the inspectors at port cities such as Mokpo and Pusan. With the police organizing the demonstrators, protest meetings and go-home demonstrations were carried out daily over a period of months.

In their protests to Rhee, U.S. officials pointed out that the U.N. Command was obligated to provide protection to the inspection teams, and expressed fears that continued demonstrations would cause bad feeling between Koreans and Americans. But Rhee had neither any compunctions about embarrassing the United States nor any sense of responsibility for grass-roots Korean-American relations. He made no move to halt the demonstrations, but instead expressed indignation.

"It has been surprising . . . to learn that Korea and Koreans have been misunderstood and wrongfully accused in connection with the demonstrations demanding withdrawal of the Communist spies of the Neutral Nations Supervisory Commission. . . .

"These demonstrations were not inspired by the Government; they are a spontaneous expression of the will and fears of the people. . . . The people have every right to demonstrate their self determination against flagrant international injustice. But we have repeatedly urged the demonstrators to conduct themselves in a non-violent and orderly manner. . . .

"Under orders, the United States Army has lined up tanks, armored cars, mortars, machine guns, rifles, chemical weapons, stones and war dogs—all this panoply of weapons to protect Communist enemies against Korean allies. Some of these weapons have been used. One Korean has been killed and almost a thousand injured, most of them not seriously. It is a great tribute to the solidarity between Koreans and Americans that our people have kept their heads and refused to resort to violence."[2]

Rhee's charges were, of course, the sheerest demagoguery.

Under continuous provocations from government-inspired demonstrators, the U.N. guards had carried out the thankless task of protecting the Communist inspectors and had themselves suffered numerous injuries from stone-throwing Korean crowds. But finally, in the summer of 1955, the demonstrations ceased. For once Rhee had exacted no concessions from the United States, and the demonstrations were no longer news in the international press. Yet neither had Washington done any more than wag a finger at Rhee, whose cheerful willingness to see South Koreans jeering at Americans across a barricade did much to damage the Korean-American solidarity which had developed during the war years.

The fact was that Rhee's frustrations had reached a point where he was almost automatically hostile to anything American. Scarcely had the demonstrations against the truce inspectors ceased when Rhee launched another attack on American representatives which culminated in the withdrawal of American Ambassador William S. B. Lacy.

In August 1955, the R.O.K. promulgated a law increasing the taxation of foreign business firms and making the new assessments retroactive to the first of the year. The businessmen affected, mostly Americans, cried foul, insisting that the retroactive aspects amounted to blackmail. When the American Embassy attempted to mediate between the business community and the R.O.K. government, Rhee made the ambassador the target of his wrath. The government press openly impugned U.S. motives in mediating the dispute, charging that the embassy seemed "bent on giving aid and comfort to those who have lied about us, cheated us, and blackened our good name."

The exact motive for Rhee's denunciation of the ambassador remain unclear. However, he was extremely sensitive to any suggestion that the United States might seek to replace him, as he himself had done away with so many subordinates who had become obstreperous. Lacy had come to Seoul from Manila, where popular rumor continued to link the election defeat of President

Quirino with his unpopularity at the American Embassy. Rhee appeared to have taken a dislike to Lacy from the start, possibly from having heard various reports concerning the Philippine elections. In any case, his anti-American campaign of 1955 had some aspects of an artificial crisis designed to "jeopardize" R.O.K.-American relations and to reflect discredit on the American ambassador.

The retroactive provisions of the tax bill were withdrawn after face-saving compromises, but not before Ambassador Lacy, in the wake of streams of vituperation in the government-controlled press, had resigned suddenly for reasons of health. The *New York Times* correspondent in Seoul, however, stated openly that health was only one factor in Lacy's resignation. Although reluctant as ever to invoke any serious sanctions against its ungrateful ally, Washington hinted its displeasure by taking six months to appoint a new ambassador.[3]

While Rhee's petulance concerning the inspection teams and his attitude in the tax dispute appeared to reflect his general frustration, it is interesting to note that they expressed themselves in a traditional Oriental manner: xenophobia. For all of his years of residence and study in the United States, when things went wrong Rhee was the first to make scapegoats of the callous foreigners who had kept him from uniting his country.

As time went on, however, Rhee's demands for a march north became less vociferous. One factor appears to have been his trip to the United States in the summer of 1954, which he appears to have viewed initially as a combination of a triumphal tour and an opportunity for sermonizing. After the usual calls and receptions—which Rhee carried off with the vigor of a man half his age—he pleaded his cause before Congress. At this crucial time, however, the Korean president's yes men let him down. No legislative body in the world could have been less enthusiastic than the U.S. Congress about any renewal of the Korean War; many of its members owed their seats to criticism of "Mr. Truman's war" in the elections of 1952. Yet Rhee delivered a speech before Congress in which he dismissed Communist China as "a monster with feet of clay" and called for a joint R.O.K.-Chinese Nationalist attack against the mainland. To Rhee there was no problem at all:

"The American Air Force as well as the Navy would be needed to insure the success of the counter-attack against the Red Chinese regime, but, let me repeat, no American foot soldier.

"The return of the China mainland to the side of the free world would automatically produce a victorious end to the wars in Korea and Indo-China, and would swing the balance of power so strongly against the Soviet Union that it would not dare to risk war with the United States."[4]

So much for Rhee the strategist; the speech met a cool reception everywhere. The *New York Times* characterized it as "unfortunate," observing that "in this speech President Rhee went beyond his customary demand for a march to the Yalu and in effect advocated an atomic world war." The aftermath to his speech brought home to Rhee, possibly for the first time, that the United States had no intention of reopening the Korean War. Yet it was characteristic of him that the response to his speech in no way shook his confidence in his own rectitude; the fault lay with the United States, which had once more lapsed into the complacency which had led to Pearl Harbor and the Korean War. In New York, in language rarely used by an official guest, Rhee observed that "the United States has not got the common guts to face the [Communist] problem. The United States is so mild in its warnings to the Communists because you don't really mean them and the Communists know you don't mean them."[5] In Philadelphia, Rhee told the Veterans of Foreign Wars that the American people must be shown "that we must fight the Communists now or later, and that the longer we wait the greater the odds against us."[6]

When Rhee returned to Korea, however, he appeared to have lost some of his fire. References to a march north were generally in a lower key, and on some occasions he would call only for the liberation of the area near the city of Kaesong, territory which lay below the thirty-eighth parallel and which had been part of the R.O.K. before the war. On other occasions he would demand a renunciation of the armistice agreement but without any specific threat of a march north.

By 1955, Korea had learned to live with the truce, Rhee's pronouncements notwithstanding. But on one side of the demilitarized zone, over half a million R.O.K. and Allied troops remained poised but a rifle shot away from a similar number of Chinese and North Korean forces. As both sides strengthened their defenses along the jagged Korean hills, they presented a concentration of military might rarely assembled at near point-blank range. As for Rhee, no one could be sure what he would do. It was an uneasy truce, indeed.

16: Rhee and Democracy

APOLOGISTS for the authoritarian aspects of the Rhee regime in South Korea have made much of the unsettled conditions there, particularly during the wartime elections of 1952. Few would agree with the contention of Rhee's admiring biographer that Rhee's sole desire in the constitutional crisis was to restore popular voting for the presidency.[1] But even among those persons critical of Rhee's conduct at that time many leaned over backwards to make allowance for the president's age and the military threat from the north. It remained for Rhee himself, in the post-armistice years, to dispel any doubts concerning the authoritarian character of his rule.

After his near-destruction of his opposition in 1952, almost four years lapsed before antiadministration forces were able to join together in any kind of cohesive group. Rhee was not entirely without opposition in the meantime, for individual attacks on the administration within the Assembly became less rare once Rhee was re-elected and martial law raised in Pusan. Not until 1956, however, were Rhee and the Liberal Party confronted with an opposition party which commanded significant popular support.

In contrast to most authoritarian regimes, South Korea was notable for a considerable degree of press freedom. It was not freedom of the press as it is known in the West, for every newspaper knew that it operated only by suffrance, and personal criticism of President Rhee was virtually unknown. Similarly, the press was permitted more leeway in Seoul, where its activities could be observed by the diplomatic corps, than in the provinces. Nonetheless, considering that constitutional safeguards concerning the individual and the free ballot were largely honored in the breach, the degree of press freedom in South Korea was somewhat remarkable.

Periodically, however, there were reminders of what could occur when a newspaper overstepped the bounds of propriety. In 1954, the anti-administration *Taegu Mail* was sacked, apparently by Liberal Party-affiliated hoodlums, after it had attacked new constitutional amendments proposed by the government. The following year, in a major *cause célèbre,* the Seoul daily *Donga Ilbo* was closed for several months after a most unfortunate typographical error in which the Korean character for "puppet" was used in place of that for "president" in a reference to Rhee. Such incidents may have represented bursts of excessive enthusiasm on the part of Rhee's henchmen rather than action taken on Rhee's orders. It is significant, however, that an instance of suppression of the press—the regime's suspension of the respected *Kyonghyang Sinmun*—was one of the events which led to Rhee's downfall.

Although Rhee had only reluctantly consented to hold Assembly elections in 1950, his opposition by 1954 was sufficiently demoralized that he had no compunctions about the elections scheduled for that year. The Liberal Party, under the methodical direction of Lee Ki-bung, had all but cleansed itself of Racial Youth Corps adherents and, though it lacked popular support, it was far better organized than any collection of opposing factions and of course enjoyed a monopoly of police support.

Confident that the 1954 elections would be easily carried by the administration, Rhee seized the opportunity to make these elections the occasion for "ratification" of a new series of amendments to the Korean constitution. First, Rhee proposed an amendment giving the voters the "right" to recall assemblymen by petition—a provision which would represent a sword over the head of every legislator, since the administration could rustle up a recall petition on a moment's notice. Secondly, Rhee proposed to abolish the post of premier, which he had come to regard with mistrust since the purge of Lee Bum-suk. Finally, he desired an amendment which would remove the two-term restriction on the number of terms which could be served by a R.O.K. chief executive.

Prior to the May elections, a combination of opposition assemblymen was still theoretically strong enough to block the amendments if they came to a vote. Rhee, however, in an action crudely analogous to that of Woodrow Wilson in 1920, made the amendments the central issue in the elections which were held on May 20, 1954. He gave official backing to all Liberal candidates who were willing to sign pledges to support the amendments. Simultaneously, in a political refinement hitherto unheard of in Korea, the Liberal Party pursued a policy of nominating only one candidate for each Assembly district. In addition, it set out particularly to defeat opposition leaders such as Shinicky and Cho Byong-ok. With the disorganized opposition running as many as ten candidates in some districts, and the police warning against the consequences of a vote against the administration, the Liberal Party carried 114 seats to 15 for the Democratic Nationalist Party and 67 for assorted independents. For the first time in its short but stormy history, the R.O.K. had an Assembly majority from one political party. The era of splinter parties had come to an end, and Rhee's opponents had been shown once again the necessity for organizing into a disciplined opposition party.

As for Rhee, the elections could hardly have gone better. Many of the independents were sympathetic to the administration, and post-election deals brought the Liberal Party total to close to 140. Racial Youth Corps adherents had been removed from the Assembly as though with a broom, yet there remained enough antiadministration assemblymen to give the Assembly some democratic trappings. Although Shinicky had been re-elected, Cho Bong-am was adjudged to have submitted his nomination petition without the required number of signatures and was forced off the ballot. Cho charged that his campaigners had all been jailed or intimidated, but he protested to no avail.[2]

In the weeks following the elections Rhee set about passing his constitutional amendments. Assured of support from a majority of the Liberal-dominated Assembly, he set about excoriating the remaining independents in order to enlist the support necessary to obtain a two-thirds majority for the amendments. Announced Rhee:

"Anyone who opposes the amendments cannot be considered anything but a traitor who is attempting to wreck the nation's drive to recover its full power. . . . I believe that any political party or groups which oppose the government should not raise any objection to the referendum clause of the bill."[3]

It was obvious that Rhee meant business, and fears of another constitutional crisis such as that of 1952 mounted. Nonetheless, with money changing hands to the tune of millions of hwan, the number of votes pledged to the administration approached the required two-thirds. But a hard core of about a third of the Assembly—comprised of militant opposition members, true independents, and a handful of legislators unenthusiastic about curbing their own prerogatives—refused to knuckle under. When the amendments finally came to a vote on November 27, the issue was still in doubt.

As the presiding officer went down the roll, excitement mounted. It soon became apparent that the margin would not be more than a vote or two either way. When the votes were tallied, the administration appeared to have suffered a humiliating defeat: with 136 votes required for a two-thirds majority, Rhee had fallen an agonizing one vote short. The presiding officer announced the amendments defeated, and the Assembly adjourned amid cries of "Mansei!" from the bill's beleaguered opponents.

But once again Rhee's enemies had reckoned without the tenacity of their redoubtable chief executive. Rhee had no intention of meekly accepting such a rebuke from the Assembly; besides, had not the people given him a mandate to change the constitution? When the Assembly convened three days later, the speaker banged for order and announced that there had been a mistake in tallying the votes on the amendment bill. Since fractional votes were to be rounded off to the previous whole number, he declared, and since there were 203 assemblymen, only 135 votes were required to pass the bill, and this number had been obtained. Opposition legislators screamed their protests, and fist fights broke out on the Assembly floor, but police moved into the hall, and the amendments were declared to have been passed.

The international press, as might have been expected, was caustic concerning this latest demonstration of Korean democracy in action. Rhee, however, was unimpressed. He had let the Assembly get out of hand once before, and his negligence had almost cost him re-election. He had no intention of allowing the Assembly to restore itself as a political force or to frustrate the very legislation he had devised to curtail its powers. As for the amendment permitting him a third term, it precluded Rhee's suffering from any of the indignities which are sometimes the lot of lame-duck chief executives in the Western democracies.

By 1954, opposition to Rhee was centered in the Assembly—the only place relatively immune from police pressures—and in certain areas of the press. Organizationally, only a demoralized Democratic Nationalist Party stood in opposition to the Liberals. Constantly under surveillance, short of funds, and with little organizational backing, the D.N.P. had fallen on hard times. The quality of its leadership, however, was a factor in its favor. Its chairman, P. H. Shinicky, was a popular figure who, to a far greater degree than his contemporaries, recognized the need for unity among opposition groups in South Korea. In Cho Byong-ok, a one-time police director under Rhee, it had a dynamic co-leader who attacked the Rhee administration with the same ardor with which he had once carried out its orders.

The year following the 1954 elections was one of soul-searching by Rhee's opponents. While they had polled a large minority of the popular vote in the Assembly balloting, they had been badly defeated, partly because of the multiplicity of their candidates. Within the D.N.P., a growing number of persons came to recognize that the old Military Government days of multiparty, multicandidate elections were over.

Among Rhee's opponents no one saw more clearly the need for opposition unity than Shinicky, the white-haired elder statesman of the Democratic Nationalists. A former Assembly speaker, and a leading independence worker in Shanghai prior to liberation, Shinicky probably came closest to matching Rhee in popular esteem throughout Korea.

In his efforts to foster a unified opposition party, Shinicky found a kindred spirit in Cho Byong-ok. When Cho had been Rhee's national police director in 1948, he had proved tough, efficient, and arrogant. He also gained such a following among the police that he was shortly fired by Rhee and thus forced into the opposition where he became one of the administration's most vocal critics. During the 1954 election campaign, in which Cho criticized Rhee's preoccupation with a march north, Cho was so badly beaten by pro-Rhee hoodlums that he annnounced his retirement from active opposition. By 1955, however, Cho was working actively with Shinicky to infuse new blood into the D.N.P. with the ultimate aim of forming a new party.

By September 1955, plans for the new party were largely complete. The new Democratic Party contained most of the old D.N.P., but also an impressive number of newcomers and independents who were led by Rhee's one-time ambassador to Washington, John M. Chang. A scholarly Catholic layman who had also served Rhee as acting premier during the war, Chang had been a popular choice for president within the Assembly in 1952. He was closely associated with the Young Korea Academy, and served to bring Western-oriented north Koreans—who had long opposed Rhee—into a party otherwise dominated by representatives of Korea's southern provinces.

As is recognized to be inevitable in Korea, the new party had its difficulties with factionalism. The more sophisticated northern Koreans looked down upon the ex-D.N.P. members, few of whom had ever traveled outside of the Orient. Former D.N.P. members resented the attempts of erstwhile independents to dominate party councils. Whatever its shortcomings, however, the new Democratic Party brought under one roof a greater number of opposition factions than would have seemed possible a few years before.

By early 1956, all of South Korea looked forward to the presidential elections scheduled for May: the first "normalized" presidential election since before the war. Unlike those of 1952 and 1954, the 1956 elections were unclouded by the threat of constitutional amendments. With Rhee regarded as certain to run again for president, and with the populace voting separately for president and vice-president, the contest promised to be an interesting clash of personalities.

Rhee himself insisted right up to the time of the Liberal Party convention that he was not a candidate. In spite of the obvious implication of the 1954 amendment permitting him a third term, 1956 brought a repetition of the ritual of 1952: "will of the people" demonstrations begging Rhee to continue in office; fasts by old men until Rhee should declare his willingness to run; and banners written in blood asking that Rhee sacrifice his personal desires for the sake of the country. Under such pressure, the aged chief executive once again allowed his name to be placed before the electorate.

While most observers regarded Rhee's own re-election as assured, there was tremendous interest in the vice-presidential contest. For with Rhee then eighty-one years old, many felt that in choosing his running mate he would be doing what he had never done in the past: anointing a successor. The belief was widespread that Rhee could not survive a third four-year term, and it was generally felt that, whatever his own feelings on this score, he would not choose another nonentity such as Ham Tai-yong as his running mate. Although Rhee's most likely choice appeared to be Lee Ki-bung, those observers who recalled his eleventh-hour dumping of Lee Bum-suk in 1952 continued to speculate concerning the possibility of a dark horse.

The general assumption was that any running mate chosen by Rhee and assured of administration support would be assured of election. Such sentiment, which was widespread even among the opposition, was based on a healthy respect for the instruments of coercion available to the administration. It underestimated, however, the extent of popular dissatisfaction in South Korea, particularly that based on economic factors. Three years of extensive foreign aid had removed the threat of starvation in South Korea and had bolstered the country's currency. At the same time, it was apparent to every Korean that tremendous fortunes were being acquired by pro-administration politicians and businessmen in the "administration" of the aid program. American aid had raised the South Korean man-in-the-street just far enough above the subsistence level for him to take time out to observe just how little foreign aid was trickling down to him.

To Liberal Party politicos who hoped that Rhee might discard Lee Ki-bung, the party convention in April 1956 came as a blow. Not only did the delegates choose Lee as their vice-presidential candidate by a near majority—after the *pro forma* renomination of Rhee—but the president came up with a statement that he was "pleased" at the convention's choice. The Democrats, on their part, prepared to go all out in the campaign. For president they nominated Shinicky, whose personal popularity and vigorous campaigning were counted on to turn out the vote. For vice-president—the race that optimistic Democrats hoped to win—the party chose John M. Chang, whose selection balanced the ticket between the two main wings of the party. But the real news appeared to be that Rhee had finally tapped a successor by giving his blessing to Lee Ki-bung, the methodical little man who had made good when offered a rare second chance to regain Rhee's good graces.

On the basis of the two previous elections, the outcome of the

14. The Revolt of April 1960: Opposition leader John M. Chang announces his resignation as vice-president four months before the end of his term in order to "ring bells of warning to the Syngman Rhee government, which is drunk with power." (*Wide World Photo*)

1956 contest appeared a foregone conclusion. Those who assumed the inevitability of a Liberal Party triumph, however, reckoned without the appeal of the Democratic Party campaign. Shinicky stumped the country, flaying the Liberal Party for its corruption, its preoccupation with unification, and its failure to better the lot of the people. Stressing the D.P. slogan, "We can't live, so let's change," Shinicky addressed one rally on the banks of the Han River which was attended by an audience variously estimated at between 100,000 and 200,000 persons. Then tragedy struck. Shinicky was en route by train to the Cholla provinces when he complained of pains in his chest and collapsed. Taken hurriedly to a hospital, he died on May 5 of a heart attack. To the credit of his Democratic Party colleagues, rumors that he had died of poisoning were denied. Shinicky's death, however, was a crushing blow to the Democratic campaign. All hopes of a large protest vote appeared to have died with the party's standard bearer.

When Shinicky's body was returned to Seoul, the train was met at the station by a good number of the great multitude which had heard him only a few days before on the banks of the Han. Tension was high, and several thousand Democrats began a march to Rhee's mansion, shouting imprecations and mourning their dead leader. Only barbed-wire barriers and heavy police reinforcements brought an end to what was perhaps Korea's first truly spontaneous demonstration since liberation.

When the voters went to the polls on May 15, Shinicky's death had not been forgotten. Out of a total of 8.7 million votes, nearly 1.8 million "invalid" ballots were cast, most of which represented votes for the dead candidate. Over 2 million votes went to Cho Bong-am, Rhee's old nemesis, some of which probably would have gone to the more conservative Shinicky, had he lived. Rhee won only 56 per cent of the vote, compared to 80 per cent in the wartime election of 1952.

Even more startling was the vice-presidential race. As the votes were counted, it soon became apparent that John M. Chang was running up large majorities in the cities, and that even in rural areas, where the Liberal Party had repeatedly capitalized on political apathy, Lee Ki-bung was barely holding his own. For once the tables had been turned: Chang, the sole Democratic candidate for vice-president, was winning only about forty-six percent of the vote, but with pro-administration ballots divided among Lee Ki-bung and three maverick Liberals, Chang appeared on his way to victory.

But would Rhee permit the election of an opposition vice-president? In Taegu, South Korea's third largest city, mysterious power failures at the counting places were followed by the disappearance of ballot boxes, and vote counters were alleged to have invalidated large numbers of Democratic votes. As Lee Ki-bung's total began to swell, the Democrats saw their victory slipping away. Tension ran high as counting was resumed and then halted once more. On the afternoon of the 19th, however, Rhee announced: "Since the will of the people has been reflected in the election, I will carry out my duty."

In terms of Rhee the man, his statement raises interesting questions. Was he completely hypocritical concerning "the will of the people," in 1956 as in 1952, or was he actually ignorant of the extent to which he had been carried away by his own ambitions when he so overworked the phrase in 1952? In any case Rhee's statement of the 19th, in effect a concession of defeat on behalf of his running mate, cleared the air. Rhee's prestige had suffered a serious setback, but it was apparent that he was unwilling to risk a repetition of the tactics of 1952 when his own position was not directly involved.

The elections of 1956 not only established the Democratic Party as a major political power, but created a situation in which the Liberal Party could be turned out in the cold should Rhee die prior to 1960. Under the circumstances, the government press, with many an allusion to America's unsuccessful experiment with separate presidential and vice-presidential elections, hinted openly at a constitutional amendment to remove Vice-President Chang from the succession. Rhee himself had no contact with his vice-president, and in effect isolated him from the functioning of the administration.

On the positive side, the elections appeared to hold up a glimmer of hope for democracy in Korea. A considerable proportion of the electorate had demonstrated a willingness to think for itself even in the face of repressive administration pressures. The beginnings of a two-party system also held out some hope for more responsible government. But in fact the seeds of the 1960 revolution had been planted, and would germinate over the next four years. The 1956 elections dramatized the rapidly ebbing popularity of the Liberal Party, if indeed it had ever enjoyed any real support. As a result of the 1956 balloting, it became apparent to Lee Ki-bung and his Liberal Party cohorts that Lee's defeat could be reversed only by use of the sternest repressive measures in 1960.

At the same time, the election of John Chang held out hope to the Korean people. If elections had been sufficiently democratic to defeat half of the administration ticket in 1956, what might 1960 bring? To educated Koreans, 1960 came to be the year in which wrongs would be righted, when overdue complaints would find redress.

Thus the goals of two diametrically opposed groups centered about the 1960 elections, and the manner in which they would be conducted.

17: The Captains and the Kings

WHEN SYNGMAN Rhee took his third oath of office at the age of eighty-one, he was the oldest chief of state in the world. His closest rival, West Germany's Konrad Adenauer, was seventy-nine. Chiang Kai-shek, often lumped with Rhee among Asia's aging statesmen, was a youthful seventy. Yet neither of these two, nor any political leader this side of the Iron Curtain, wielded more influence over his realm than did Rhee.

A brief comparison of the Rhee government with Nationalist China is not without some interest. Both were parts of countries divided as a result of the East-West struggle, and both were heavily dependent on American support. Both were widely regarded as authoritarian regimes which reflected the backgrounds and aspirations of their strong-willed leaders. There were also, however, some interesting differences.

In the international field, South Korea's position was considerably stronger than that of the Nationalists. Not only does the Republic of Korea continue to control roughly half of the Korean peninsula, but the rival North Korean regime has yet to be recognized by any country outside the Communist bloc. Although it has been prevented by Soviet vetoes from joining the United Nations, South Korea's international position appears considerably more assured than that of the Nationalists, the latter's representation on the Security Council notwithstanding.

Although both South Korea and Formosa have been thought of as monolithic regimes, there are also interesting comparisons in the domestic field. For all his penchant for personal rule, Rhee was instrumental in giving South Korea the form of a democratic republic. That the R.O.K. government under Rhee was modeled to a considerable extent on the United States was reflected in the four-year presidential term, a nominal separation of powers among the executive, legislature, and judiciary, and a constitution which bristled with guarantees patterned after the American Bill of Rights. In tolerating any opposition at all, Rhee felt that he was pointing South Korea along the pattern of the Western democracies.

In contrast with the R.O.K., the Nationalist government on Formosa was and is recognizable as an offshoot of an essentially Oriental background. Rather than follow Rhee's example in permitting a controlled opposition, Chiang has institutionalized one-party rule by the Kuomintang, justifying it on the grounds that China requires a period of tutelage prior to full self-government. Although neither regime has been noted either for honesty or governmental efficiency, the structure of the R.O.K. government has reflected Rhee's years abroad while that of Formosa appears scarcely to have changed since the days of Sun Yat-sen.

After the initial shock had worn off, the period after the 1956 elections found Rhee in a relatively beneficent mood. He rarely threatened a march north, and never with his former vehemence. He preferred to content himself with less specific promises of eventual unification, though he stoutly maintained that unification could only be achieved through force. Rhee bridled at the thought of John Chang in the vice-presidency, but he made no move to push through a constitutional amendment to remove him from the succession. While disgusted with Lee Ki-bung's election showing, he continued to rely on Lee as chairman of the Liberal Party and speaker of the National Assembly.

Nonetheless, the fact remained that because of Rhee's advanced age the presence of Chang in the vice-presidency had an unsettling effect on the local political scene. In September 1956, a would-be-assassin wounded Chang slightly as he was leaving a D.P. rally in Seoul, thus prompting him to go into virtual seclusion for the next two years. No one openly accused Rhee of complicity in the shooting, although Chang's assailant presumably felt he was carrying out Rhee's wishes. The attempted assassination was sufficiently embarrassing to Rhee that, in contrast with the manner in which Colonel Ahn was turned out to pasture following the assassination of Kim Koo, Chang's assailant was put to death.

To the long-suffering Korean people, Chang became a hero, and for Rhee time was rapidly running out. But in his hillside mansion Rhee worked in the morning, napped in the afternoon, and puttered in his garden. An appalling amount of his time was spent on trivia, including the signing of documents and the greeting of visitors, with the latter invariably being subjected to the party line on Japan's designs for the reconquest of Korea. The R.O.K. cabinet met at varying intervals, but it was prone to go for long periods without meeting at all. It was characteristic of the Rhee administration that the cabinet had little function in policy-making: it merely listened to Rhee expound it. The fact was that South Korea had no policy-making mechanism as such. The party line was laid down by Rhee, who presumably acted at times aided by the advice of his wife or Lee Ki-bung. The extreme insecurity of tenure under Rhee discouraged any frank exchange of views between the president and his ministers.

The rapid turnover among Rhee's subordinates, exemplified in the fact that the R.O.K. had no less than sixteen home ministers in the first ten years of its existence, reflected more than the ordinary vicissitudes of working for a quick-tempered octogenarian. Rhee was aware, at least to some degree, that his age and position tended to isolate him from the day-to-day workings of government, and he was quickly suspicious of anyone accused of building up a personal following. His one failure to check a rival early in the game, he felt, had necessitated the portentous Racial Youth Corps purge. Never again did Rhee allow a subordinate to gain so strong an independent following as he had Lee Bum-suk in 1952.

Unfortunately, Rhee's brand of one-man rule did not make for efficiency in government. He had neither the time nor the energy to make all the necessary decisions, yet he would not delegate authority to others. When this paralysis of the decision-making process was compounded by Rhee's penchant for cabinet reshuffles, the result was chaos. Rhee's own biographer has acknowledged:

"Everyone who has a problem, whether he be a Korean, an American, or a representative of one of the several international organizations in Korea, tries if he can to get the direct attention of the president. When the government was first organized, with lines of authority not clearly defined, cabinet ministers developed the habit of bringing to President Rhee for final decision a great many of the problems with which they had to deal. This habit has persisted unduly—partly because of Dr. Rhee's own nature; partly because cabinet officers have been frequently changed, so that there are always new and inexperienced ones; and partly because Korea has been beset during the short life of the republic by a mass of problems too acute to permit of anything but top-level decision."[1]

The problem was not so much that many matters required top-level decisions—indeed, Rhee's qualifications in fields such as economics and defense were marginal—as that his subordinates lived in fear of his catching them in a lapse. Because the timid ministers were simultaneously afraid to venture a decision on their own and fearful of incurring Rhee's wrath by bringing him inconsequential matters, all important decisions were made by the president while unimportant matters were often not acted on at all.

Rhee's relative isolation from day-to-day Korean politics made him an ideal foil for administration politicos bent on discrediting their rivals. His prejudices and quick temper made it easy for members of his entourage to hint that so-and-so was pro-Japanese, or that such-and-such had been seen in a tea room with a member of the opposition. The perhaps inevitable isolation of anyone of Rhee's age was heightened by the atmosphere around Kyungmudae, which was not unlike that of the old Korean court: flatterers, informers, and syncophants enhanced their own positions by channeling their views to the president's aging ears.

Although Rhee's fundamental outlook on matters such as Japan, communism, and his political opponents was virtually incapable of change, his more moderate tone on the issue of unification demonstrated that he was capable of facing reality when forced to do so. In the absence of strong outside pressures, however, any changes in policy were usually dictated by propaganda considerations. Late in 1958, Rhee announced that the R.O.K. was willing to resume "normalization" talks with Japan; in effect, to resume the talks broken off by the South Koreans in 1953. But R.O.K. demands were so outrageous that the Japanese, desirous of getting rid of their Korean residents, turned to North Korea for discussions concerning the disposition of pro-Communist residents fearful of repatriation to South Korea.

Ever the nationalist, Rhee found time to champion causes which would not have had a claim on the time of another chief executive. As president, Rhee pushed vigorously for a simplified Korean alphabet, *hangul,* for everyday use. Though he was himself an expert in Chinese calligraphy, he could appreciate the hours and years required to learn the various ideographs. Hangul, a phonetic alphabet rather than a means of representing whole ideas by symbols, is far easier to learn and more adaptable to the expression of new ideas. Rhee was far from alone in his interest in modernizing his native language: in common with other Eastern nations, the Communists were active proponents of language reform in both China and North Korea.

One of Rhee's less practical campaigns concerned the reforestation of South Korea. First the Japanese, and after 1945 the Koreans, had ruthlessly exploited Korea's once-luxuriant forests with virtually no attempt at conservation or reforestation. An already serious lumber shortage became a disaster during the Korean War, when the ebb and flow of battle ravaged whole sectors of the country and left hills barren of vegetation.

In the bitter Korean winters, the choice for many Koreans was one of finding wood with which to heat their shacks or of freezing. Rhee, however, had little concept of the desperate straits in which his people found themselves, and in his espousal of reforestation he treated the cutting of trees as a serious crime. This did not wholly prevent the reaping of firewood, but it did mean that the people who most needed the wood now had to pay off the police who caught them in the act of reaping. Rhee himself made tree-planting a police responsibility all over South Korea, and come Arbor Day, would himself take spade in hand to plant a symbolic tree by some dusty road.

President and Mrs. Rhee took a notable step in their personal lives in 1957. Over a period of years they had both become attached to Speaker Lee Ki-bung and his wife. The Assembly speaker had attained a degree of personal friendship with the Rhees apart from his role as the president's political lieutenant. In a move which was regarded as having political as well as personal significance, the Rhees announced on March 26—the president's eighty-second birthday—the adoption of the Lees' elder son, Lee Kang-suk. There was little public reaction to the adoption, which was of a type not unusual in the Orient. But the stage was now set for the final act of Lee's ill-starred career. He had successfully merged his personal and political fortunes with those of his friend and benefactor. He little realized that the final reckoning would bring disappointment, despair, and ultimately death.

The political lull that marked the Korean scene after the 1956 elections came to a stormy close toward the end of 1958. In the Assembly elections earlier in the year, the Democrats had scored notable gains, raising their total number of seats from forty-seven to eighty-two. A considerable proportion of the Liberal Party, who allowed carefully for the advantages with which their party went into any election, read the handwriting on the wall: unless the trend towards the Democrats could be halted, Rhee himself might be defeated in 1960 and the Liberal Party consigned to oblivion. Although Rhee was incapable of imagining himself in such a desperate plight, his aides were not, and it was probably they who set about obtaining the passage of legislation which helped the Liberals to carry the 1960 elections.

In November, the administration made its move. Alleging a need for new anti-Communist legislation, Liberal assemblymen introduced with Rhee's blessing a series of revisions to South Korea's already stringent security laws, amendments which provided for death sentences or heavy prison terms for vague crimes such as "disseminating Communist propaganda" and which could obviously be adapted to any South Korean election campaign. Opposition groups attacked the new bill strenuously as a transparent attempt to lump all criticism of the Rhee regime with Communist propaganda and as a device for use in the 1960 presidential elections. After the Democrats conducted a six-day sitdown strike against the bill in the Assembly, Liberals took matters into their own hands on Christmas Eve by calling in Assembly guards to clear the opposition from the floor. When numerous Democrats resisted, fist fights broke out, and opposition legislators were carried bodily out of the hall and locked in the basement. The Liberals remaining then passed twenty-two bills, ranging from the key provisions of the controversial security law to a bill which abolished elections for local offices.

The security law affair was a useful reminder that there was a limit to which democracy could be permitted in South Korea, even in peacetime, and that when Liberal Party control of the country was threatened, that limit had been reached. If Rhee appeared to have been less the instigator of the security law controversy than a beneficiary, he nonetheless countenanced and defended the Liberal tactics in the Assembly as well as approved the bills which were passed. Nor was he above rubbing salt in his enemies' wounds: when a newsman asked him in January 1959 if he thought he would run again, Rhee broke precedent by acknowledging that he "thought" he would.

Rhee himself maintained stoutly that the new security law was aimed solely at the Communists, not at his political opponents. Other observers, who had heard this before, saw in the manner in which the security bill was passed a return to the roughhouse tactics of 1952. Whatever Rhee's attitude, by 1959 it was no longer his wishes alone which counted. The syncophants and hangers-on who rode the administration gravy train no longer shared Rhee's assumption that he remained first in the hearts of his countrymen. They sought desperately for a means to insure their future for four more years by securing Rhee's re-election and that of a Liberal vice-president.

The king was not dead; indeed, he was very much alive. His voice still shook with emotion on the subject of Japanese depredations in his country. His glance could still inspire fear in a balky minister. But Rhee was no longer using people so much as people were using him. His courtiers were already making plans to forestall the day when his death would turn them out into the cold. If the security law episode proved nothing else, it demonstrated how by dredging up one of Rhee's old bogies—in this case his fear of Communist infiltration—Liberal Party diehards could obtain his approval of whatever legislation they might require.

18: The Deluge

THE PASSAGE of the National Security Law and the incarceration of the assemblymen brought gloom to the Democratic Party. Four years previously they had felt that the election of John Chang as vice-president might lead to their gaining control of the government by means of Rhee's demise. As time went on, not Rhee but their hopes had died. Yet Rhee's advanced age remained a factor mitigating against any revolution, particularly in the absence of a vigorous opposition leader. Vice-President Chang, although active in party affairs, continued to live in virtual seclusion.

At the Democratic convention in February 1960, it was generally agreed that the party's nominees for the presidential elections would be Chang and Cho Byong-ok. As in 1956, however, neither of the two opposition leaders was anxious to "take on the champ." The execution of Cho Bong-am had provided one more reminder of the hazards faced by anyone with the temerity to challenge Rhee. At the same time, no one believed Rhee to be immortal, and in 1960 the vice-presidency figured even more prominently in political calculations than in 1956.

It is possible that even at convention time the Democrats saw the handwriting on the wall; that there was to be no repeat of their vice-presidential upset, and that they could only hope to poll a sufficient vote in defeat to preserve their party unity for the long pull. In any case, the Democratic convention was surprisingly lacking in factional bitterness and resulted in the choice of Cho

Byong-ok to run against Rhee and John Chang to attempt to succeed himself in the all-important vice-presidency. The administration party, as expected, "nominated" Lee Ki-bung to run with Rhee.

The campaign was scarcely underway when Cho Byong-ok was taken seriously ill and sent to the United States for hospitalization. Then, in a move that was widely interpreted as an attempt to take advantage of Cho's incapacitation, Rhee scheduled the elections for March 15 instead of the customary date in May. Whatever his motive, Rhee's action proved unnecessary. Cho died at Walter Reed Hospital of complications resulting from an abdominal operation a full month before the elections. As in 1956, the opposition had a dead man as its presidential candidate.

Unlike 1956, however, when the police greatly underestimated the extent of antiadministration feeling, the administration was now on its guard. Opposition workers were repeatedly arrested and beaten; at least one was admittedly killed while under arrest prior to the balloting. Hoodlum members of the "Anti-Communist Youth Corps" let it be known that they would be in alternate voting booths on election day to see how each citizen between them cast his ballot.

When the votes were counted after March 15, it was found that 88.7 per cent of the 11,230,000 ballots were for Rhee; the remainder—characterized as "invalid"—were almost all for Dr. Cho. But the eye-opener was the vice-presidential race. The official figures showed Lee Ki-bung defeating Dr. Chang by 8,225,000 votes to 1,850,000—a remarkable reversal of their 1956 contest. On top of the lopsided vote count came more embarrassment, for the head-knocking by Rhee's police was far from bloodless. Twenty persons died in election-day violence, usually in connection with demonstrations against the fraudulent vote count, and many more were injured.

The handling of the elections confirmed the worst fears of Rhee's opponents. But it was even more of a blow to the Korean populace. Although in terms of skulduggery involved it was no more a travesty than Rhee's re-election by the Assembly in 1952, by 1960 the Korean people expected to have a real voice in their own government. Their reaction was explosive.

As was to be expected, the Democrats in the National Assembly protested the elections vigorously. On March 18, they began a boycott of Assembly activities, and subsequently they went through the motions of seeking an injunction to invalidate the elections. According to the Democrats, a number of votes equal to forty per cent of the total electorate had been fabricated and used to pad the Liberal Party vote. But there was no reason to think that this protest would be any more effective than any other of the Assembly demonstrations which had marked the turbulent course of democracy in South Korea.

When the first post-election disturbances flared, they stemmed from popular indignation rather than the efforts of any political group. Clashes in Seoul between students and police on April 7 were followed by bloody riots in the southeastern port of Masan three days later. The cause of the riots was a minor incident by Korean standards; it seemed that the Masan police had arrested a sixteen-year-old pro-opposition student on election day, shot him, and thrown his body into the bay. But its repercussions were to be considerable.

For nearly a month after the elections the atmosphere in South Korea's cities was one of uneasy tension. Spontaneous demonstrations, usually student-led, occurred in Pusan and Taegu as well as Seoul and Masan. On April 16, Rhee issued his first statement concerning the demonstrations: they were instigated by the Communists.

Rhee was blind to the true extent of discontent among his countrymen, and yet he had been blind for years. There was still no sign that the popular wrath would take any more concrete form than it had in the past. Students had demonstrated before the gates of Kyungmudae in 1956, and the Republic still lived.

Were not the army and the police, who so often held the key to events in Korea, still loyal? If Rhee was complacent, so were many of his more realistic lieutenants.

A hazy sun rose over the dull gray that was downtown Seoul on Tuesday morning, April 19. At first it seemed like business as usual as the A-frame porters moved about in search of their day's trade. But this was not a day like other days, and an ominous quiet hung over the city.

For Seoul's politically conscious, antigovernment students, this was to be the day of the Great Protest. At Seoul National University, in the northeast sector of the city, student agitators began to stir up excitement and to call for a rally. As the day went on, and students from high schools and universities alike converged on downtown Seoul, it became apparent that student leaders had planned a major demonstration.

By mid-day, over 100,000 persons, with students in the majority, milled in the streets. As the mob gained in strength, it turned its ire on objects of special hatred. Jeering, shouting students burned five police stations, sacked the offices of the administration organ *Seoul Sinmun,* and broke into Liberal Party headquarters. In many areas of the city there was little opposition to the rioters; many policemen fled their posts and went into hiding.

But there were others to take their places. When the crowd surged past the old Capitol building and turned up the road leading to the presidential mansion they found the way blocked by police. Student spokesmen claimed that they wanted only to present a petition to the president, but the police ordered them to disperse. When the demonstrators continued to press towards Kyungmudae, the nervous police at first fired tear gas shells. When the crowd still refused to break up, police fired volley after volley into the milling students.

By early afternoon a state of martial law had been declared in Seoul. R.O.K. Army troops moved into the city at nightfall to enforce the seven o'clock curfew. But the Rhee regime had nothing

15. Lee Ki-bung, his wife, and his sons, Lee Kang-uh and Lee Kang-suk. In a suicide pact consummated on April 28, Lee Kang-suk, the son adopted by the Rhees in 1957, shot his parents, his younger brother, and himself as an act of atonement for the misfortunes that had befallen their chief. (*Wide World Photo*)

further to fear that night; there were 115 dead throughout the city and over 1,000 wounded or injured, and those who escaped unscathed returned to their homes. Smoke from the burned-out buildings spiraled upward as the troops dispersed through the city.

Within the administration, the traditional gestures were made. Rhee's cabinet moved to resign and to take the blame for the near-revolutionary state of the country. Rhee, however, showed no indication that he comprehended what was going on about him:

"It is almost unbelievable that any element of the patriotic Korean people, to whom I have devoted my life, could act in such a way [as the demonstrators did]. However, this is not the time to discuss causes or to attempt the placing of the blame. The first task is the full restoration of law and order so that the necessity of martial law no longer exists."[1]

Rhee had scarcely expressed his surprise concerning the demonstrations when he found his position undermined from an unexpected source. The United States, which had suffered silently with Rhee for so many years, chose this occasion to deliver a stinging rebuke to its old ally. In a sharp note released simultaneously in Seoul and Washington, the State Department charged the Rhee administration with using "repressive measures unsuited to a free democracy." According to Secretary Herter, the R.O.K. government "should, in its own interest, take necessary and effective action aimed at protecting democratic rights of freedom of speech, of assembly, and of the press, as well as preserving the secrecy of the ballot." The United States had belatedly joined the side of the angels. In Seoul, crowds cheered as the American ambassador returned to his embassy from Kyungmudae.

In the wake of the bloodletting of April 19, an uneasy truce prevailed. In the National Assembly, the emboldened opposition denounced the resignation of Rhee's cabinet as insufficient and demanded new elections. In the teahouses, Washington was rumored to be urging Rhee to undertake a broad range of political reforms, including the holding of new elections. For Rhee and his courtiers, the most dreaded moment of all had arrived: the United States had indicated publicly that it was no longer willing to support the *status quo* in South Korea.

Nonetheless, Rhee continued to temporize. He invoked a full range of face-saving devices designed to appease the anger of the mob. On April 22, he called in for consultation a group of elder statesmen to "advise" him concerning the crisis; his advisors, all junior to him by about twenty years, included the recent mayor of Seoul, Huh Chung; ex-Foreign Minister Pyun Yong-tae; and Rhee's erstwhile strongman, Lee Bum-suk. The following day Rhee offered to the people a counterproposal. He would yield to demands for a governmental reorganization, and restore the post of premier, in return for a restoration of order. Vice-President-elect Lee attempted to aid his chief by means of an announcement that he was "considering" retiring from public life.

Rhee's gesture met with some approval among Liberals in the National Assembly, where restoration of parliamentary government would mean greatly increased power for the legislature. But he had directed his concessions in the wrong direction. It was not the Assembly which was demanding reforms, but the populace at large. And there was yet no indication from Kyungmudae of a willingness to effect the type of top-to-bottom housecleaning desired by the students. On April 24, Rhee announced that he was severing all his ties with the Liberal Party, but there was still an air of equivocation about his statements. Would not the Liberal Party continue to do his dirty work?

Rhee's vacillation inevitably brought new protests from the street. On April 25, the crowds once more surged into downtown Seoul. The soldiers made every effort to avoid violence, but there were still sufficient police in evidence to insure bloodshed. Once again police and police stations were a primary target of the mob, but the demonstrators were now united on a single theme: Rhee must resign. When the day ended there were fifteen more dead to be listed on the casualty roll of the revolution, and at least two hundred injured. To the panic-stricken presidential mansion, however, came rumors that the Army would refuse to fire on any crowd seeking Rhee's resignation.

By the morning of the 26th it was apparent that Rhee's offer of governmental reforms would not satisfy the populace. From Kyungmudae came new concessions: the government would call new elections for both the presidency and the vice-presidency in addition to making the cabinet responsible to the Assembly. Rhee had asked Lee Ki-bung to give up all his official positions. Finally, Rhee stated that he was willing to resign "if the people [so] desire." In the southern city of Pusan, 300,000 demonstrators demanded Rhee's resignation while at the same time jubilant students in Seoul celebrated his seeming offer to abdicate.

It is impossible to say whether Rhee still expected the people to rally to his cause. But whereas in 1952 there was a well-oiled administration machine to turn out "will of the people" demonstrations on Rhee's behalf, in April 1960 the rats were leaving the sinking ship. On Wednesday the 27th, a crowd of nearly 100,000 gathered outside Kyungmudae in anticipation that Rhee would announce his resignation. But no word came, and the celebrations in the city gave way to an ominous quiet. In the National Assembly, where nearly two-thirds of the members were nominally members of the administration party, a motion demanding Rhee's immediate resignation was passed without debate.

Rhee had named a new cabinet following the resignation of his ministers in the wake of the outbreaks on April 19. Since Vice-President Chang had resigned in protest over the election, the second-ranking member of the administration was Foreign Minister Huh Chung, an American-educated administrator who had served Rhee at different times as a cabinet minister, acting premier, and mayor of Seoul. The inscrutable Huh had broken with Rhee on sufficient occasions to avoid being closely identified with the regime. Although there is no reason to believe that Rhee appointed him foreign minister with the idea that he would end up as acting president, the choice appears to have been a fortunate one.

When Rhee finally forwarded his resignation to the National Assembly on the afternoon of the 27th, it came as an anticlimax. The public accepted the fact of Huh's accession to the acting presidency, reassured by his promise of new elections. There was still a feeling of unreality about the whole revolution. Would Rhee, who had fought tooth and nail to retain his position for twelve years, step down without further bloodshed? What would be the attitude of the United States towards a government headed by anyone other than Syngman Rhee? And what of Lee Ki-bung?

In a cottage on the grounds of Kyungmudae, the last act of a personal tragedy was enacted by the family of Lee Ki-bung. For years Rhee had encouraged Lee in the unrealistic hope that he might succeed him as president, and Lee had done his chief's bidding whatever the cost to his own popularity. Now there seemed to be but one act of contrition by which Lee might accept responsibility for the misfortunes which had befallen his chief. On the morning of April 28, as Rhee prepared to leave the presidential mansion, a guard found the Lee family—the speaker, his wife, his younger son, and Lee Kang-suk, the son adopted by the Rhees—dead as the result of a suicide pact.

The suicide of Rhee's trusted lieutenant left the country momentarily stunned. But interest soon turned to the caretaker government and the manner in which it would meet the demand for new elections. Huh promised reforms in police administration, closer supervision of American aid, and efforts to improve relations with Japan. As Syngman Rhee moved into his ancestral villa, overlooking Seoul National University, South Korea finally realized it had ushered in a new chapter in its history.

"The dark era of tyranny is past. The reign of the gangsters is over. Remember two things: the students' death and United States aid. Now is the time to calm down and rebuild the country."[2]

19: Korea's Syngman Rhee

AS THIS chapter is written, the caretaker government of Huh Chung has been in office less than a month. There is still no indication of who will be elected to succeed Syngman Rhee when elections are held later this summer. Regardless of who is chosen, however, and regardless of whether he will have to share his powers with a premier, the path of Rhee's successor will be a difficult one.

Revolution is heady wine, and defiance of authority, once successful, can be habit-forming. For twelve years South Korea lived under Rhee's authoritarian rule, hoping for the opportunity for a change. Now the change is a fact. The question is whether the installation of a new government, together with the initiation of political and institutional reforms, can bring a restoration of stability. This is a question which only the Korean people can answer.

As for Rhee, his tragedy is that a lifetime devoted to his country should have left so little of lasting value. Nonetheless, for half a century he could truly be called Mr. Korea. It is difficult not to feel a certain awe for a redoubtable old patriarch who in six or more decades of rough-and-tumble politics neither gave nor asked for quarter. Even late in life he could command an audience by the mere force of his personality and the mystique which surrounded a lifetime spent in behalf of Korean independence. In his dedication as in his demagoguery, Rhee was a true revolutionary.

This quality of personal magnetism, apparent even in his early years, did much to shape the course of Rhee's subsequent political career. Prior to becoming president of South Korea he had had virtually no experience as an executive or administrator. However, he was never far from a speaker's platform, and can be said to have spent much of his first seventy years in denouncing his enemies from a lectern. When he became a chief of state late in life he could scarcely accept the fact that he was at the top of the heap. Like a punch-drunk prize fighter, he continued to strike out at his old opponents.

It is a truism that the revolutionary hero, the leader of the crowd, is often ill-suited by temperament to lead his people as head of their government. So it was with Rhee. His admirers attempt to represent him as the sagacious statesman, wise as becomes one of his years, who has clung steadfastly to his lifelong objectives while others faltered along the way. The facts, however, do Rhee less credit. His rashness and impetuosity—typified by his release of the prisoners of war, the threats to march north, and the blanket accusations against his opponents—bespeak the revolutionary zealot rather than the statesman.

An unfortunate aspect of Rhee's shortcomings is that few revolutionaries have had such a promising background. Following the collapse of the Independence Club in 1905, Rhee was one of a fortunate few who were able to make their way to friendly shores. Entering America from one of the most backward countries in the world, Rhee had four decades in which to prepare for his return. His academic studies and his travels gave him a chance to absorb political thought in both the United States and Europe.

In the bitter infighting among exile factions in Hawaii, Rhee was exposed to the techniques of survival among political groups whose weapons were conspiracy and assassination. It is unfortunate that he learned so much of political infighting and so little of enlightened statesmanship. In any case, when he returned to Korea to fulfill his role as Father of his Country, he took a blackjack along. One does not have to wonder how Woodrow Wilson, the hero of Rhee's youth, would have regarded the Kochang massacre, the

Racial Youth Corps gangsterism of 1952, or the 1960 presidential elections.

If Rhee had a single fatal flaw it was his egotism, which made it all but impossible for him to accept criticism, or to change his mind once he had made it up. By 1945, the decades spent in the service of Korea had led him to identify himself almost totally with the future of his country. When the U.S. government failed to fly him back to Korea after liberation, it was somehow a Communist plot; similarly, General Hodge's failure to turn South Korea over to Rhee proved the general to be either blind to the wishes of the Korean people or a Communist dupe. Rhee's attitude towards Korean affairs was perhaps summed up in his purported remark upon taking charge of the National Society in 1946. Observed Rhee: "I shall take over the society and run it on a purely democratic basis. I shall appoint all the other officials."[1]

Rhee's ambition to become president of a united Korean republic was a logical outgrowth of his essentially messianic outlook. His popular support stemmed both from respect for his past labors for Korean independence and from his ability to dramatize the general desire for unification. Unfortunately, he was too often a victim of his own circular reasoning; he was quite capable of viewing the popular desire for unification as demonstrating approval for his policies and administration. It is understandable that he was frustrated by the Communist occupation of North Korea and by the Allied strategy in the Korean War, which he felt denied him the opportunity to unify his homeland. This wartime frustration possibly accounts for the fact that many of the excesses of his regime were most pronounced in the years from 1952 through 1954, when he still held hopes that he might extend his domain to the Yalu.

As a wartime leader, Rhee communicated his own fire and patriotism to the Korean people. Indeed, the admirable manner in which the then septuagenarian recovered from the initial shock of the Communist invasion to become a rallying point for his people blinded many observers to his obvious shortcomings as a chief of state. If Rhee symbolized to his people the struggle for unification, his appeal to Washington was that of an uncompromising anti-Communist at a time when his breed were harder and harder to find. As a result, Rhee enjoyed firm support from the United States even at times when he was working as best he could to undermine American policy concerning Japan, a Korean armistice, or the development of democracy in Korea. He was the subject of overgenerous praise from so many American officials who visited Korea that he found his own self-esteem confirmed at every hand.

Although Rhee's physical vigor was and still is remarkable for one of his years, the fact remains that he became president at a time when he was far beyond the prime of life. Rhee's very age made him impatient; if Korea was to be unified in his lifetime, there was no time to lose. In addition, the advancing years had underscored his sensitivity to criticism and unreceptiveness to change. Rhee looked upon Korea in the 1950's in terms of the same shibboleths as he had at the turn of the century: fear of the Japanese, fear of the Russians, and faith in his own righteousness. Moreover, by his eighth decade he had devoted so much of his life to Korea that he was incapable of bringing any perspective to bear on the East-West struggle apart from the Korean issue. He paid lip service to the concept of a Pacific anti-Communist alliance, but was unable to bring himself to include Japan. He was completely incapable of understanding that some nations, even in the Free World, were largely indifferent concerning the question of Korean unification.

Rhee's two great shortcomings, his egotism and the inflexibility which characterized his old age, made him the most difficult imaginable ally with whom to deal. He insisted on making all important decisions himself, yet could not be counted on to carry out his pledged word. He knew little of economics, but could not be shaken of his conviction that changes in the hwan-dollar exchange rate were a major cause of inflation. It is unfortunate but not entirely surprising that Rhee's shortcomings were not compensated for by advice from trustworthy subordinates. Rhee was never one to seek advice which might be at variance with his own preconceptions, while his periodic tantrums bred a sense of servility in his advisors. South Korea's shortage of capable public officials was aggravated by Rhee's insistence on yes men, and in time he drove most self-respecting officials out of the government.

For all his shortcomings, however, Rhee was not merely a stubborn old tyrant in a position of power. He was an extremely astute political tactician, a fact which was on continuous display during his rise to the top of the cutthroat world of Korean politics. And on the international scene, Rhee parlayed Korea's status as a victim of Communist aggression into a degree of support from the United States which makes any new Communist attack unlikely.

By any standard, Rhee's success in identifying the defense of his country with U.S. interests is remarkable. In 1950, South Korea's general economic poverty, lack of natural resources, and extreme strategic vulnerability were doubtless factors which contributed to its exclusion from the Truman administration's proclaimed defense perimeter in the Pacific. Three years later, with all these drawbacks multiplied tenfold, Rhee's domain was bound to the United States through a mutual security pact. While Rhee did not control the international events which brought about this metamorphosis, he played his hand with great skill. To impress public opinion in the United States, Rhee made speeches which bristled with references to Woodrow Wilson, the Magna Carta, and the rights of man. Aided considerably by the American press, Rhee did a remarkable job of selling himself as the courageous "little man" who never gives up, a veritable one-man Fourth of July complete with Confucian overtones. Divorced from any ethical considerations, Rhee's march north blackmail—and it is difficult to treat it as anything else—paid off handsomely for

South Korea. Not only did Rhee obtain his mutual security pact, which remains his country's greatest bulwark against any new aggression, but he exacted aid commitments which made his country the largest single recipient of American aid.

For all his considerable success in dealing with the United States, it was on the domestic scene that Rhee's domination was complete up to the very end. While in the international field he was never to persuade his allies to unify Korea on his behalf, in the domestic arena there were no such frustrations. His rise to the top after World War II was rapid and virtually without interruption. Once in the presidency, he benefited, as he had all along, from a shortage of capable opponents. Acknowledgment of his pre-eminence by most rival political factions made it easier for him to manipulate the factional infighting which distinguishes Korean politics.

Wielding the power that he did, Rhee might have been the Kemal Ataturk of Korea. But he had no program for his country apart from his preoccupation with unification. It is significant that even prior to the Korean War the record of Rhee's administration was virtually barren of legislation designed to improve the economic lot of the people. When Rhee was not agitating for unification he was busy consolidating his position in the presidency. When his ministers were doing anything at all, they were accommodating the financial interests whose political contributions supported the Liberal Party machine.

Although Rhee was doubtless in ignorance of many of the deeds committed in his name, his own sins were much more than those of omission. His deliberate use of the police as a major prop for his regime perpetuated one of the most loathsome features of the Japanese occupation. His repeated flouting of the constitution gave the fledgling Korean republic a legacy of instability and disregard for legal safeguards.

One of the most damaging by-products of the Rhee regime was its effect on public morality. While Rhee himself was aloof from the graft and thievery about him, his willingness to support his underlings, whatever their crimes, attracted to the administration the worst elements in politics and commerce. In the years after the Korean War the regime became increasingly dependent on the police and the government-sponsored mass organizations for its very survival. The loyalty of these instruments, in turn, could be maintained only from the proceeds of illegal trade with Japan, rigged auctions of aid goods, and the thievery of U.S. military supplies.

Rhee's was not the first, and it may not be the last, corrupt government in Korea. It is unfortunate nonetheless that the country's first Western-trained chief executive did so little to raise the moral tone of government. For all his early training, Rhee's rule in South Korea had less in common with democratic rule as it is understood in the West than with the tithes, decrees, and vendettas of the Yi dynasty court. Had Rhee been less exalted by his allies during the Korean War, and had American aid been made conditional on certain standards of behavior, Rhee might have been pressured into reforms which would have made the revolution of 1960 unnecessary. However, he was never called upon to account for his excesses in the early stages, but instead was repudiated by the United States at a time when his administration was on the verge of collapse, and when his usefulness to the Free World cause was more than outweighed by his liabilities.

Rhee's successor must inevitably face an awesome array of problems. He must satisfy the democratic aspirations of the Korean people, aspirations which have been frustrated for many years. He must seek an accommodation with Japan which will enable South Korea to live with its Free World neighbor on at least correct terms with respect to diplomacy and trade. He must teach his people to demand honest government and to work for the economic rehabilitation of their country.

Not all of these problems had to be the lot of Rhee's successor. Some were of Rhee's own manufacture; others, he permitted to develop; all were aggravated at different times on his own whim. But when their president had at long last been overthrown, there was much that the students were willing to forget. They chose to remember, instead, the tales learned at their mother's knee of the venerable sage who had come from across the sea to lead his children out of the wilderness. One youth spoke for many as Rhee's limousine moved slowly out of the Kyungmudae grounds, possibly for the last time. "He is now a patriot," said a student. "His resignation proved it. We would not have forgiven him had he not stepped down."

16. Syngman Rhee and Mrs. Rhee, after a secret plane flight from Seoul, arrive in Honolulu on May 29, 1960, and are welcomed by Korean Consul General C. C. Oh. Although the Rhees explained that they had come to Hawaii to rest and recuperate and that they would return to Korea, it appeared that the drama of Syngman Rhee's career had reached its epilogue. (*Wide World Photo*)

Epilogue

Special to the *New York Times,* by Robert Trumbull:

SEOUL, Korea, Thursday, April 28—Huh Chung, who became President when Syngman Rhee resigned yesterday, turned today to the task of curbing the ills that led to the overthrow of the Rhee Government.

He charted a course of democratic reforms at home and of an improvement in relations between this troubled 12-year-old republic and the United States and Japan. . . .

Taking over the Government immediately upon the President's resignation in the confused aftermath of bloody student-led uprisings against the Rhee regime, 63-year-old, tall, scholarly Mr. Huh said that he would attempt to straighten out what he called "mismanagement and waste" in the gigantic United States aid program here. He also said at a news conference that he would seek to unravel South Korea's tangled affairs with Japan.

Mr. Huh . . . promised new Presidential elections, superseding the discredited March 15 poll that led directly to Dr. Rhee's downfall.

By the time the election date is set, he indicated, the form of government may have been changed to eliminate the office of Vice President while placing executive power in the hands of a Premier and leaving the President as more or less a figurehead.

Notes

CHAPTER 1

1. Cornelius Osgood, *The Koreans and Their Culture* (New York, 1951), p. 203.

2. Robert T. Oliver, *Syngman Rhee: The Man behind the Myth* (New York, 1954), pp. 13–15. The absence of material on Rhee's early years has forced the author to rely, to a greater degree than he would desire, on Oliver's "official" biography. Since Oliver enjoyed access to papers provided by Rhee himself, the book is of value in its noncontroversial areas.

3. Rhee's decision to enter the Paichai School appears to have been a difficult one for him since it suggested a repudiation of his mother's Confucian teachings. In later life he related how "she took me by the hand and said, 'My child . . . you are going to become a *Chunchuhak Koon* (God-cult fanatic), are you not?' 'No, mother,' I assured her, 'I am too wise to believe what they say. Have you ever known a scholar to become a believer of that religion?' These remarks relieved her a little, but did not entirely free her mind from anxiety." *Ibid.*, pp. 60–61.

4. Frederick M. Nelson, *Korea and the Old Orders in Eastern Asia* (Louisiana State University, 1946), pp. 210–12.

5. Donald G. Tewksbury, ed., *Source Materials on Korean Politics and Ideologies* (Institute of Pacific Relations, New York, 1950), p. 12.

CHAPTER 2

1. F. A. McKenzie, *The Tragedy of Korea* (London, 1908), p. 84.

2. *Source Materials,* pp. 12–13.

3. Oliver, *op. cit.,* pp. 46–47.

4. *Ibid.,* pp. 49–50.

5. Nelson, *op. cit.,* p. 244.

6. Oliver, *op. cit.,* p. 61.

7. *Ibid.,* pp. 340, 57–59. Only a few excerpts from *The Spirit of Independence* have been translated into English, and those are in Rhee's "official" biography. The fact that the Rhee government never issued a translation tends to confirm that it is not a mature work.

8. Nelson, *op. cit.,* pp. 250–51.

CHAPTER 3

1. Oliver, *op. cit.,* pp. 86–87.
2. *Ibid.,* p. 96.
3. Andrew J. Grajdanzev, *Modern Korea* (New York, 1944), p. 35.
4. Oliver, *op. cit.,* p. 104.
5. *Ibid.,* p. 111.
6. *Ibid.,* p. 121.

CHAPTER 4

1. Oliver, *op. cit.,* p. 125.
2. Resolution of the Comintern Executive Committee in December 1928, quoted in Walter Kolarz, *The Peoples of the Soviet Far East* (New York, 1954), p. 40.
3. From *The New Administration in Chosen* (July 1921), an official publication of the governor-general of Korea, quoted in Grajdanzev, *op. cit.,* p. 66.
4. Syngman Rhee, *Japan Inside Out* (New York, 1941), p. 8.
5. *Ibid.,* pp. 168, 176.
6. *Ibid.,* p. 22.

CHAPTER 5

1. Oliver, *op. cit.,* p. 179.
2. U.S. Department of State press release, June 8, 1945, quoted in George M. McCune, *Korea Today* (Cambridge, Massachusetts, 1950), p. 42.
3. Oliver, *op. cit.,* p. 189.
4. Louise Yim, *My Forty-Year Fight for Korea* (New York, 1951), p. 223.
5. Samuel Rosenman, ed., *The Public Papers and Addresses of Franklin D. Roosevelt, 1942* (New York, 1950), p. 476.
6. Cordell Hull, *Memoirs* (New York, 1948), Vol. II, p. 1596.
7. U.S. Department of State, *The Conferences at Malta and Yalta: 1945* (Washington, 1945), p. 770.
8. Oliver, *op. cit.,* p. 195.
9. U.S. Senate, *The United Sates and the Korean Problem* (Washington, 1953), pp. 2–3.
10. Carl Berger, *The Korea Knot* (Philadelphia, 1957), p. 49.

CHAPTER 6

1. E. Grant Meade, *American Military Government in Korea* (New York, 1951), p. 54.
2. Oliver, *op. cit.,* p. 213.
3. Berger, *op. cit.,* p. 58.
4. McCune, *op. cit.,* p. 50.

CHAPTER 7

1. McCune, *op. cit.,* p. 81.
2. *New York Times,* January 24, 1947.
3. *Ibid.,* May 23, 1947.
4. *Ibid.,* February 25, 1947.
5. R.O.K. Office of Public Information, *The Constitution of Korea* (Seoul, 1954), p. 12.
6. Chung Kyong-cho, *Korea Tomorrow* (New York, 1946), p. 203.

CHAPTER 8

1. McCune, *op. cit.,* p. 243.
2. *Ibid.,* p. 250.
3. *Ibid.,* p. 355.
4. Oliver, *op. cit.,* p. 271.
5. *New York Times,* May 8, 1949
6. Walter Millis, ed., *The Forrestal Diaries* (New York, 1951), p. 273.
7. *New York Times,* October 29, 1948.
8. McCune, *op. cit.,* pp. 241–42.
9. Yim, *op. cit.,* pp. 303–4.
10. *New York Times,* June 28, 1949.

CHAPTER 9

1. Harry S. Truman, *Years of Decision* (New York, 1955), p. 383.
2. *New York Times,* January 13, 1950.
3. *Source Materials,* pp. 145–46.
4. Rutherford M. Poats, *Decision in Korea* (New York, 1954), p. 1.
5. *Ibid.,* p. 9.
6. Harry S. Truman, *Years of Trial and Hope* (New York, 1956), p. 336.
7. *Ibid.,* p. 337.
8. Poats, *op. cit.,* p. 22.

CHAPTER 10

1. Poats, *op. cit.,* p. 69.
2. Leland M. Goodrich, *Korea: A History of U.S. Policy in the United Nations* (New York, 1956), pp. 133–34.
3. *Ibid.,* p. 139.
4. Poats, *op. cit.,* p. 91.
5. *Ibid.,* p. 100.
6. Matthew B. Ridgway, *Soldier* (New York, 1956), pp. 210–11.
7. Berger, *op. cit.,* p. 132.
8. Truman, *Years of Trial and Hope,* p. 455.

CHAPTER 11

1. *New York Times,* May 28, 1952.
2. *Ibid.,* May 30, 1952.
3. *Ibid.,* June 12, 1952.
4. *Christian Science Monitor,* June 5, 1952.
5. Henry S. Hayward, in the *Christian Science Monitor,* June 17, 1952.
6. *Washington Post,* June 30, 1952.
7. *Christian Science Monitor,* June 30, 1952.
8. George Barrett, in the *New York Times,* August 6, 1952.
9. *Ibid.*

CHAPTER 12

1. Melvin B. Voorhees, *Korean Tales* (New York, 1952), pp. 154–55.
2. Poats, *op. cit.,* p. 226.
3. *Ibid.,* pp. 216–17.
4. Mark W. Clark, *From the Danube to the Yalu* (New York, 1954), pp. 257–58.
5. Berger, *op. cit.,* p. 160.
6. Clark, *op. cit.,* pp. 269–70.
7. *Ibid.,* p. 272.
8. Poats, *op. cit.,* p. 263.
9. Clark, *op. cit.,* p. 275.
10. R.O.K. Office of Public Information, *Korea Flaming High* (Seoul, 1954–55), Vol. I, pp. 35–36.
11. Clark, *op. cit.,* p. 281.
12. *Ibid.,* p. 286.
13. *New York Times,* June 12, 1953.
14. Clark, *op. cit.,* pp. 287–88.

CHAPTER 13

1. *Korea Flaming High,* Vol. I, pp. 91–92.
2. U.S. Department of State, *The Korean Problem at the Geneva Conference* (Washington, 1954), p. 7.
3. *Korea Flaming High,* Vol. I, p. 139.
4. Robert Allen, in the *New York Times,* December 14, 1953.

CHAPTER 14

1. *Korea Flaming High,* Vol. II, pp. 16–17.
2. Clark, *op. cit.,* pp. 156–57.
3. *Korea Flaming High,* Vol. II, pp. 16–17.

CHAPTER 15

1. *Korea Flaming High,* Vol. II, p. 10.
2. *Ibid.,* pp. 91–94.

3. *New York Times,* November 27, 1955.
4. *Ibid.,* July 29, 1954.
5. *Ibid.,* August 1, 1954.
6. *Ibid.,* August 2, 1954.

CHAPTER 16

1. Oliver, *op. cit.,* pp. 285–86.
2. *New York Times,* April 28, 1954.
3. United Press, Seoul, October 22, 1954.

CHAPTER 17

1. Oliver, *op. cit.,* p. 277.

CHAPTER 18

1. *New York Times,* April 24, 1960.
2. *Chosun Ilbo,* independent Seoul newspaper, quoted in the *New York Times,* May 1, 1960.

CHAPTER 19

1. Frank Gibney, "Syngman Rhee: The Free Man's Burden," *Harper's,* February 1954.

Bibliography

DOCUMENTS

McCune, George M., and Harrison, John A., eds.: *Korean-American Relations: Documents Pertaining to the Far Eastern Diplomacy of the United States,* University of California, 1951

R.O.K. Office of Public Information: *The Constitution of the Republic of Korea,* Seoul, 1954

——, ed.: *Korea Flaming High* (speeches and addresses by Syngman Rhee during the years 1953–55), 2 vols., Seoul, 1954–55

Rosenman, Samuel, ed.: *The Public Papers and Addresses of Franklin D. Roosevelt, 1942,* New York, 1950

Tewksbury, Donald G., ed.: *Source Materials on Korean Politics and Ideologies,* Institute of Pacific Relations, New York, 1950

U.S. Department of State: *The Conferences at Malta and Yalta: 1945,* Washington, 1945

——: *The Korean Problem at the Geneva Conference,* Washington, 1954

U.S. Senate: *The Korean War and Related Matters,* Washington, 1955

——: *The United States and the Korean Problem,* Washington, 1953

MEMOIRS

Clark, Mark W.: *From the Danube to the Yalu,* New York, 1954

Hull, Cordell: *Memoirs,* 2 vols., New York, 1948.

Millis, Walter, ed.: *The Forrestal Diaries,* New York, 1951

Pyun, Yung-tai: *Korea My Country,* Seoul, 1954

Ridgway, Matthew B.: *Soldier,* New York, 1956

Truman, Harry S.: *Years of Decision,* New York, 1955

——: *Years of Trial and Hope,* New York, 1956

Yim, Louise: *My Forty-Year Fight for Korea,* New York, 1951

GENERAL STUDIES

Berger, Carl: *The Korea Knot,* Philadelphia, 1957

Chung, Henry: *The Russians Came to Korea,* Washington, 1947
Chung, Kyung-cho: *Korea Tomorrow,* New York, 1956
Dennett, Tyler: *Roosevelt and the Russo-Japanese War,* New York, 1925
Feis, Herbert: *The China Tangle,* Princeton, 1955
Goodrich, Leland M.: *Korea: A History of U.S. Policy in the United Nations,* New York, 1956
Grajdanzev, Andrew J.: *Modern Korea,* New York, 1944
Harrington, Fred H.: *God, Mammon, and the Japanese,* Madison, Wisconsin, 1944
Hulbert, Homer B.: *The Passing of Korea,* New York, 1906
Kolarz, Walter: *The Peoples of the Soviet Far East,* New York, 1954
Latourette, Kenneth S.: *A Short History of the Far East,* New York, 1946
McCune, George M.: *Korea Today,* Cambridge, Massachusetts, 1950
McCune, Shannon: *Korea's Heritage,* Rutland, Vermont, and Tokyo, Japan, 1956
McKenzie, F. A.: *The Tragedy of Korea,* London, 1908
Meade, E. Grant: *American Military Government in Korea,* New York, 1951
Nelson, Frederick M.: *Korea and the Old Orders in Eastern Asia,* Louisiana State University, 1946
Oliver, Robert T.: *Syngman Rhee: The Man behind the Myth,* New York, 1954
Osgood, Cornelius: *The Koreans and Their Culture,* New York, 1951
Poats, Rutherford: *Decision in Korea,* New York, 1954
Rhee, Syngman: *Japan Inside Out,* New York, 1941
Treat, P. J.: *The Far East: A Political and Diplomatic History,* New York, 1928
Voorhees, Melvin B.: *Korean Tales,* New York, 1952

PERIODICALS

Baldwin, Roger N.: "Our Blunders in Korea," *The Nation,* August 2, 1947
Deane, Hugh: "The Death of Lyuh Woon-hyung," *The Nation,* September 6, 1947
Hodge, John R.: "With the U.S. Army in Korea," *National Geographic Magazine,* June, 1947
Gibney, Frank: "Syngman Rhee: The Free Man's Burden," *Harper's,* February, 1954
"An Interview with Syngman Rhee," *U.S. News and World Report,* March 7, 1952

Index

Numbers in italics indicate references to photographs and captions.